A Balfour Book printed and published by Photo Precision Limited, St. Ives, Huntingdon, England.

Red Arrows

by **Ray Hanna** photographs by **Arthur Gibson**

IMPRIMIS PRAECEPTA

Foreword

by Air Vice-Marshal I. G. Broom CB, CBE, DSO, DFC, AFC.

Ray Hanna was in his last full season as leader of the Red Arrows when I became Commandant of the Central Flying School, the team's parent unit. He epitomised all the qualities which one looks for in an aerobatic team leader.
An outstanding pilot with several thousand hours' flying on a wide variety of aircraft.
Firm and decisive in his orders. A leader in every sense of the word. A man others would follow without question, for he led by example.
He demanded the highest form of self-discipline from his men. They responded so magnificently that he built the Red Arrows into the most famous formation aerobatic team in Europe—and probably in the world.
Today their name is a household word.
The modern formation aerobatic team consists of highly disciplined, experienced and mature pilots—real professionals, not the daredevil type of pilot portrayed in Hollywood films.
The average age of the Red Arrows is normally around 30, and Hanna himself was over 40 when he relinquished command of the team.
Training is the keynote of the team's success. In this book, Hanna takes the public behind the scenes and gives a glimpse of the way in which the team is trained during the winter months in order to reach the immaculate standard which thrills us all each summer.
Wherever they go in their scarlet-painted, British-built Gnats, their formation flying brings honour to their country. It feels good to be British when watching the Arrows perform abroad. I confess that my eyes have frequently been moist with pride when scores of thousands of spectators in foreign countries have risen to their feet, waving their programmes and spontaneously applauding the performance of the Arrows. In the United Kingdom, enquiries about service in the Royal Air Force show a marked rise wherever the Arrows perform, and every season letters pour into the Central Flying School from all over the world, expressing appreciation of their faultless performances.
Typically, Ray Hanna gives generous recognition to the part played by the ground crew in producing the aircraft in perfect condition for each performance. I know that no praise is too high for them. When the performance finishes and the thousands of spectators drift away, the pilots can relax but the dedicated ground crew may well work continuously through the night to ensure that the Gnats are in perfect order for the next flight.
The hours that these ground crew work would astonish the general public. No trade union hours for them—and no extra pay either for them or the pilots. Yet there is no shortage of volunteers for the team or the supporting ground crews. The competition to become a member of this crack aerobatic team is tremendous, and the only reward lies in the satisfaction and pride which come from membership.
In this book, Ray Hanna repeatedly stresses that teamwork is the cornerstone of the Red Arrows' success. It is therefore appropriate that the book itself is also very much a product of teamwork. Arthur Gibson is one of the foremost aviation photographers in the United Kingdom. Up to 1973, he had flown more than 150 sorties with a succession of Red Arrows teams, having flown for the first time with Hanna's team in 1967.
I saw Hanna and Gibson working together; they formed a great team. They would discuss plans in minute detail before their flights so that they knew precisely the sort of photographs they were seeking. Some of the photographs which resulted from that partnership are reproduced in the following pages. Hanna and his men produced a ballet of movement in flight; Gibson captured it for posterity on film and in the still photographs which help to make this book a fine tribute to a unit which has brought so much credit to the Royal Air Force and to Britain.
The fame and influence of that unit reach far beyond the boundaries of the United Kingdom and even of Europe. At the 1972 Farnborough Air Show, for example, a member of the visiting Chinese delegation was asked if he had seen anything at the show which he would like to buy.
"Yes", he said. *"The Red Arrows".*

The official crest of the RAF Central Flying School is painted on the side of the fuselage of each of the Red Arrows' aircraft.

Cockpit ambassadors

People sometimes refer to the Red Arrows as "the premier aerobatic team of the Royal Air Force". Or as "the RAF's leading aerobatic team". Or as its "official aerobatic team". Well-meant phrases, all of them—but all wrong.

The truth is really much simpler: since 1965, the Red Arrows have been The Aerobatic Team of the Royal Air Force.

There are, of course, other flying display teams in the RAF, both at home and overseas, all with some sort of official standing. Normally they represent a particular station or unit. Only the Red Arrows represent the whole of the RAF—and that means that, at overseas displays, they represent Britain itself.

The Arrows are, in fact, unique in a number of ways. For instance, it was only when they were formed that the RAF had an aerobatic team whose full-time job was display flying. Before that, the chosen team was usually drawn from an operational squadron of Fighter Command, and its display function was secondary to its operational duties.

Again, no other team has ever filled the premier aerobatic position for so long.
In 1969, when the Red Arrows were already in their fifth year, it was announced that they would continue for a further five years. Barring unforeseeable developments, therefore, they will remain Britain's aerial ambassadors until the mid-seventies.
By then, the Hawker Siddeley Gnat—the aircraft they have flown ever since their formation—will itself be nearing the end of its career in RAF service.

It is hard to imagine that any future team will better the length of the Red Arrows' tenure of office. It is also hard to imagine, though, that the day could ever come when the RAF would willingly be without an aerobatic display team.

Most major air forces field an aerobatic team. On the Continent, in particular, there is a tremendous public following for aerobatic displays. At large air shows in Europe and in Britain, there can often be teams from the USA, France, Italy and Belgium, and many other countries have teams which, although perhaps less widely seen, still "show the flag" to a wide public.

"Showing the flag" is very much part of the job of any air force's aerobatic display team, and the pilots who take part in international displays have sometimes been called "Cockpit Ambassadors". The official brochure of the French team, La Patrouille de France, defines the team's role in terms which leave no doubt about this side of their function. Loosely translated, it says:
"To show to a wide public in France and overseas the quality of equipment in service, the training of the pilots and the merit of the specialists, to arouse career-interest among the young—such are the principal objectives pursued by the Armée de l'Air in forming a national aerobatic team".

It is a definition which could equally well be applied to the Red Arrows or to any national team. The world being what it is, prestige still counts for quite a lot, and there is prestige in excelling in the international arena of formation aerobatics—prestige not just for the team and its individual members, but also for the Service and the country they represent.

At home, displays by teams like the Red Arrows provide the ordinary taxpayer with one of his few chances to see something of the work of the RAF. Nobody would doubt, either, that the team's public displays help to stimulate recruiting. When the armed services have to compete with commerce and industry to attract the right type of young men, recruitment needs all the stimulus it can get.

Overseas, the value goes beyond simply impressing the ordinary taxpayers of other nations. For every emergent country, an air force is an important element of defence. Every air force has to get its training

The Red Arrows looping in 'Diamond 9' formation.

Formation loops are one of the oldest of aerobatic team manoeuvres. Above, five Sopwith Snipes of the first Central Flying School team flying a 'follow-my-leader' loop at the Hendon air display in 1921. Below, a quartet of SE5As — among the few World War 1 fighters to continue into peacetime service with the RAF in the early 1920s — inverted at the top of a loop during a display.

somewhere, and only the larger countries have the resources to provide pilot-training to the standards essential for today's sophisticated combat aircraft; apart from anything else, it is only these countries which actually have the latest types of combat aircraft so that their pilot-training is always to a higher standard.

Most smaller countries therefore look to larger, friendly nations to train at least a nucleus of their pilots. Providing that training is one way of establishing a position of influence with a developing air force, which can often be important in the context of aircraft procurement as well as in more abstract terms. Quite a few countries look to Britain for pilot-training—and it is hard to think of a better way of demonstrating that the UK knows how to train good pilots than the displays of flying skill provided by the Red Arrows.

On balance, then, the outlay on the equipment, organisation and operation of a "national" aerobatic team is far from being a waste of money. It can even be said that it is a national investment.

Apart from all these considerations, though, formation flying is in itself an important element in the pilot-training syllabus.

There was a time when men were satisfied with simply lifting an aeroplane off the ground, flying it in a few sedate turns, and putting it safely back on the ground in one piece. That period lasted about as long as it took to develop aircraft which would really fly, as distinct from just defying the law of gravity. Once aircraft became really controllable and men were really at home in the sky, aerobatics began to be developed.

At first, they were individual aerobatics—sometimes simply for kicks, sometimes to demonstrate the structural qualities of the aeroplane. Formation flying came with the emergence of the aeroplane as a military machine and the establishment of sizeable flying units.

The original object of formation flying was to enable each machine in a flight or squadron to bring the maximum firepower to bear for its own defence. These close flying formations have virtually vanished from tactical and operational flying, just as the hollow squares and other rigid battle formations employed by infantry have vanished. But from those early formations and their cautious, cumbersome manoeuvring there has developed the whole art of precision formation aerobatics.

In the very early days, individual aerobatics also had a very real practical value in actual combat, and many manoeuvres were, in fact, developed by combat pilots. The principles of air-fighting have perhaps changed relatively little, but greater pilot proficiency and technical development of aircraft and their armament have tended to diminish the value of pure aerobatic ability. All the same, aerobatics continue to be taught because there is no better way of giving a pilot confidence in both himself and his aircraft, particularly when manoeuvring near the limits of the aircraft flight envelope. Similarly, formation aerobatics help to weld a collection of individual pilots into a team and give them confidence in their fellow pilots.

The development of formation aerobatics into public displays was an almost inevitable progression. Apart from demonstrating that public money was paying good dividends in terms of skill and efficiency, displays provided a stimulus for pilots to achieve the highest possible standards.

From 1920 onwards, aerobatic teams were a staple feature of most air displays in Britain. Standards were high from the beginning: the 1920 team of five Sopwith Snipes from the RAF's Central Flying School looped and rolled in formation and flew inverted. The following year, five SE5As of the Royal Aircraft Establishment introduced a formation spin. Always there has been a constant pressure to improve and diversify the repertoire; nobody has ever been satisfied with just keeping up with the Joneses, everybody wants to go one better!

Compared with the tight, mathematically precise jet formations of today, early biplane formations looked relatively loose and ragged. Lower speeds, however, allowed manoeuvres impossible for jet formations, such as the mass 'opposition pass' (above) by 18 Armstrong Whitworth Siskins, flying in six 'Vics' of three, at Hendon in 1929. The looseness of the early formations is more

So innovation has always been the order of the day, and many of the formations and manoeuvres featured by today's acrobatic teams have their roots in far earlier display sequences. Looking back, one tends to get a slightly despairing feeling that there is nothing new under the sun.

In 1926, for example, the public could "listen in" to instructions wirelessed from the ground to nine Gloster Grebes of No 25 Squadron, flying in sections of three.
A year after that No 41 Squadron's nine Siskins were "doing it to music", performing their aerobatics and formation changes to relayed music.

"Synchro" flying made its bow at least as early as 1929 when two Grebes of A&AEE, Martlesham Heath, gave a synchronised display at the Hendon Air Show, trailing smoke. A year later, No 43 Squadron's nine Siskins introduced a new twist by flying in sections of three aircraft with their wings linked by breakable cord.

Special paint schemes also began to be used in the '30s. The 1931 CFS team of five Gipsy Moths had red markings on their upper wings so that spectators could more easily see when they were inverted (which was most of the time!).

Smoke was also used to embellish displays, a notable "set piece" being the "Prince of Wales Feathers" manoeuvre used by the 1932 Bulldog team.

Formation changes in the course of display sequences were also featured by No 25 Squadron's three Hawker Furies in 1935, and the following year No 1 Squadron had a fourth Fury "in the box" just far enough below the leader to avoid his slipstream. This team, incidentally, displayed abroad as well as in Britain.

evident in the photograph (below) of five Moths of the 1931 CFS team in inverted orbit, apparently during a private performance for the occupants of Blenheim Palace!

Competition between aerobatic teams has always stimulated innovation. In the 1930s, several teams – including the 1936 trio from No 19 Squadron (above) – developed the technique of flying with wingtips linked by breakable cord. About the same time, special paint schemes were introduced. Avro Tutors of the Central Flying School (below) had striped upper wing surfaces to enable spectators to distinguish more easily when aircraft were flying inverted.

Increased power, performance and controllability brought a tightening up in aerobatic formations. A notable example is this formation from No 1 Squadron in the 1930s, flying perhaps the most beautiful of all biplane fighters—the Hawker Fury, a lineal ancestor of the Red Arrows' Gnat.

The process of continuous evolution which had characterised the development of formation aerobatics in the biplane era came to an abrupt end with the approach of war. Whether it would have continued unbroken is, in any case, problematical.

The high manoeuvrability of the biplane fighters had been one of their main fighting strengths. With the advent of the faster, relatively less "handy" monoplane fighters, there was inevitably less emphasis on manoeuvrability and more on speed (both in climb and in level flight) and on weight of firepower. Air-fighting tactics had already begun to change, and aerobatics were taking the more or less subsidiary place in the training syllabus which they hold today.

Even before 1939, there were some head-shakings and prophecies of doom about the impracticability of mounting aerobatic displays with the faster aircraft which were coming into service. It seems ironic now that aircraft like the Spitfire should have made people doubt whether it would be possible—for reasons of speed and manoeuvrability—to keep a display within the confines of an airfield. If those pessimists could have foreseen the coming of jet fighters, they would certainly have decided that display flying was all over bar the shouting. Yet formation aerobatics not only re-started after the war but have been raised by the world's jet teams to a new pitch of perfection, both as a demonstration of flying skill and as a public spectacle.

The first RAF jet team consisted of three Vampires from the Odiham Fighter Wing in 1947. In the following year, a Vampire team from No 54 Squadron was enthusiastically received by spectators in the USA and Canada, and it became apparent that it was possible to devise display routines which—though different in style from the pre-war biplane displays—exploited the qualities of jet aircraft and appealed to the same kind of public.

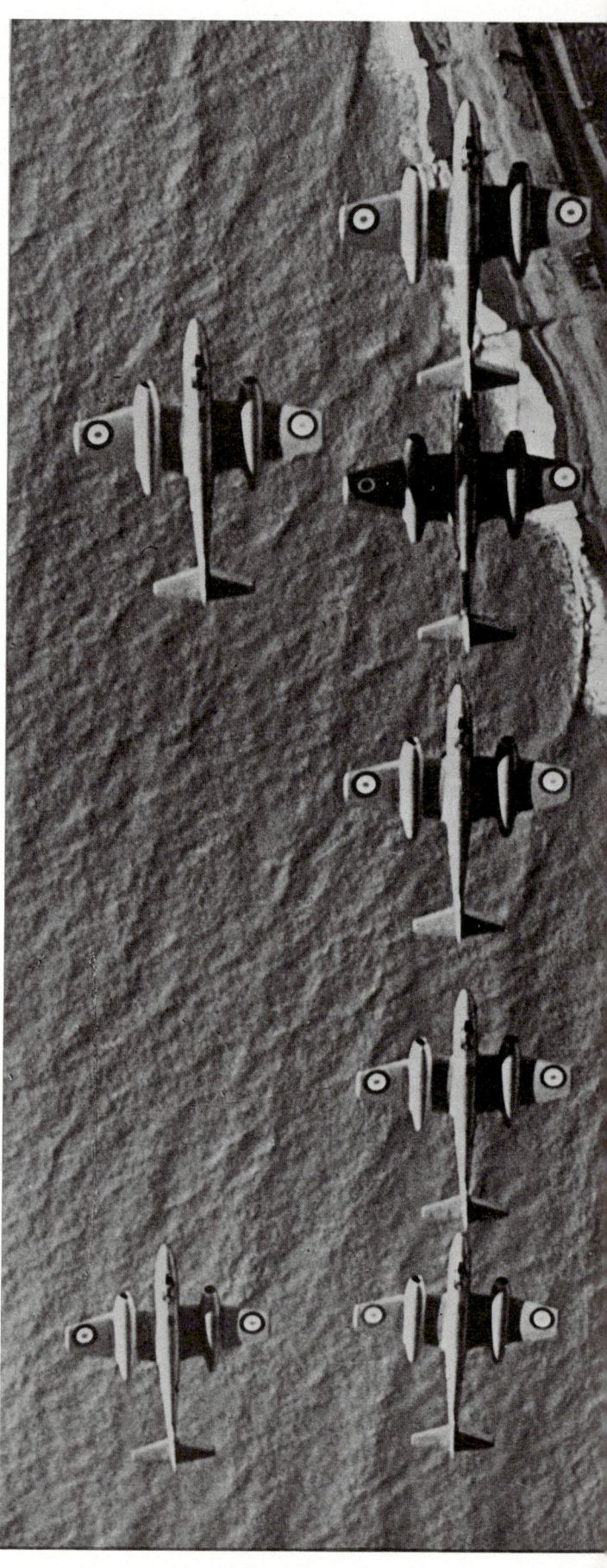

When formation aerobatics were resumed after World War 2, doubts about the feasibility of public displays with jets were soon laid to rest. First jet to be used by RAF teams was the de Havilland Vampire, and No 54 Squadron's five-strong formation (left) featured coloured smoke in its displays. Gloster Meteors were also used for a brief period, and No 1 Squadron included a particularly apt formation (centre) in its display sequences in the early 1950s.

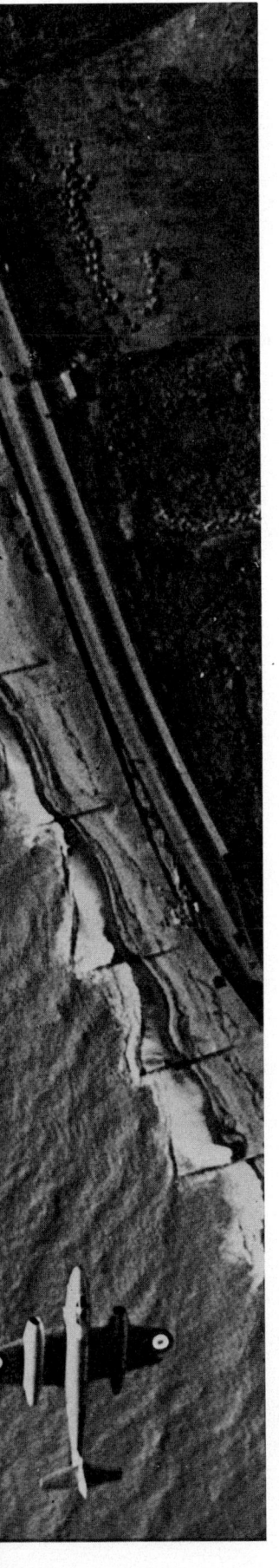

Vampires remained the RAF's formation aerobatics aircraft up to 1950, with No 72 Squadron putting up a seven-strong formation and No 54 Squadron's five-aircraft team using smoke. Meteors took over from the Vampires for a while, but the really definitive development in RAF jet formation aerobatics came with the Hawker Hunter.

The first Hunter teams were those of Nos 43 and 54 Squadrons, but the squadron with which the Hunter will always be identified when it comes to formation acrobatics is No 111 Squadron. "Treble-One" is unquestionably one of the classic "big names" in this field. At first, four of its Hunters shared the stage with the other teams but in 1957 "Treble-One" became the RAF's premier team and gave its Hunters their famous all-black finish. Curiously enough, the name by which they became famous—"The Black Arrows"—originated not in Britain but in France, where one of their displays won them the description of "les flèches noires".

If any one team was the "father" of modern formation aerobatics, it was the Black Arrows. It is probably true to say that, until they came on the scene, jet formations had to some extent been borrowing from memories of the pre-war displays and trying to make jet aircraft fit pre-war piston-engined patterns, rather than starting from first principles and devising displays which would show off the particular characteristics inherent in jet aircraft, such as speed and power.

Clearly, no modern jet fighter or trainer can be flown in a formation display at anything like its maximum speed because it would then be really impossible to keep the action in front of the spectators. But there is no denying the sense of power communicated to spectators by a formation of jets. The higher speeds, as compared with piston aircraft, give the watchers an impression of smoothness and precision of control quite different from the impression conveyed by the piston-engined biplane formations.

The Hawker Hunter proved to be one of the classic jet formation aircraft. Among the first RAF Hunter aerobatic display teams was this four-ship formation from No 43 Squadron.

First jet aerobatics team to get a firm hold on public interest and imagination was the famous Black Arrows of No 111 Squadron. 'Treble-One' – regarded by many as the fathers of modern formation jet aerobatics – thrilled the 1958 Farnborough air show crowds with a 22-Hunter loop in 'Pterodactyl' formation. It was the largest jet formation looped up to that time.

To some extent, one always felt aware with the biplanes that one was watching separate aircraft, flown by separate individuals; with leading modern jet teams, it is sometimes difficult to appreciate that the aircraft are separate units. The formation is integrated to a far greater extent than even the pre-war Furies and Bulldogs linked by lengths of cord. The whole formation functions like one huge, powerful machine—an extension of the leader's aircraft. It is unlikely that Squadron Leader Roger Topp, the Black Arrows' first leader, ever thought about his team's display in those terms; he was probably concerned only with the practical problems of devising a display sequence which showed off the Hunter's characteristics to the full.

In doing so, he had an advantage none of his predecessors had enjoyed: for the first time in postwar years, one aerobatic team was retained for a period longer than a year. The benefits soon became apparent. "Treble-One's" performance grew steadily smoother and more professional. There was less need to concentrate on basics and more opportunity to experiment and innovate. New manoeuvres and new formations were introduced, perhaps the most memorable of them being the 22-Hunter loop during the 1958 Farnborough Show. It was the first time so large a formation had been looped, and it drew spontaneous applause from the appreciative crowds.

No 111 Squadron continued as the premier RAF team—with Peter Latham taking over command from Roger Topp—until 1961 when the "Blue Diamonds" of No 92 Squadron under Squadron Leader Brian Mercer replaced them. The Blue Diamonds introduced a number of new formations but probably their most important move was to split their 16-strong formation into two groups for some sections of their display. Following the split, a formation of either seven or nine aircraft was constantly "on stage", and this gave the programme considerably greater coherence and flow.

When the Blue Diamonds of No 92 Squadron took over from the Black Arrows in 1961, they set a new pattern by splitting their 16-Hunter formation into sections of nine and seven aircraft (above) – a practice which gave their performances increased continuity and flow. The Tigers of No 74 Squadron (below) had the distinction of being the first RAF team to display Mach 2 aircraft. Their Lightnings are shown in a 'Diamond 9' roll.

There is no doubt that the whole approach of the RAF teams to display flying had now become more professional. There was an increased appreciation of the need to consider display content and presentation from the point of view of the *public* spectator rather than that of pilots or knowledgeable observers. Performances were being planned as continuous spectacles, rather than a series of intermittent, though impressive, set-pieces punctuated by what radio broadcasters call "dead air".

What is often forgotten, I think, is that the Hunter teams and their leaders developed this increased professionalism in display flying while their aerobatic role was still very much subsidiary to their squadrons' operational role.

The early 1960s saw a series of changes in the aerobatic teams. No 74 Squadron, re-equipped a year earlier with Lightnings, had the distinction of being the first RAF team to display Mach 2 aircraft in tight-formation wing-overs and rolls. In 1962—now named "The Tigers"—they combined with the Blue Diamonds to present a co-ordinated display.

Another Lightning team—No 56 Squadron's "Firebirds"—took over in 1963 but their tenure of office marked the end of an era in RAF formation aerobatics. Henceforward, the RAF was to adopt the policy of drawing its formation teams from units other than the operational fighter squadrons and using trainer aircraft instead of high-performance combat aircraft.

Initially, this change must have been a disappointment to many public spectators. Up till then, they had been able to feel that they were watching not only the most advanced pilots but also the Service's most advanced aircraft. It was, however, a change forced on many air forces around that period by sheer practical necessity—the French, for instance, switched from fighters to Fouga Magisters in the same year (1964) as the RAF changed from Lightnings to Jet Provosts.

The problem was simply that mounting aerobatic teams of high-powered, high-performance, operational aircraft imposed burdens which no air force could justify or sustain. Operational aircraft were being developed to higher and higher performance standards and inevitably becoming more sophisticated and more costly. Apart from the sheer expense of the operation, there must always be potential danger in forcing complex, sophisticated aircraft to perform for protracted periods in conditions far removed from the environment for which they were designed. High standards of training and discipline may minimise the risk of accident, but they cannot prevent airframe fatigue life being eroded far more rapidly than is economically allowable.

The first team of jet trainers in the RAF was composed of six Jet Provost Mk 4 aircraft of the Central Flying School—a unit which had played a prominent role in RAF formation display flying since the very earliest days. Named "The Red Pelicans", this team gave as polished a display as its predecessors but, after formations of nine Lightnings and 16 or even 22 Hunters, it would have been surprising if the six Jet Provosts had not seemed rather tame. The sense of power was gone and no one—however generously inclined—would say that the JP was in itself the most aesthetically beautiful of aircraft!

Fortunately, though, for the considerable public following built up by the RAF teams, that most cherished of British solutions —an ideal compromise—was at hand.

And it came about, as British compromises are apt to do, almost by chance—chance, though, which was helped along by one man's drive, determination and personality.

The era of fighter squadron formation teams ended in 1964 when the Red Pelicans of the Central Flying School, flying Jet Provost trainers, became the RAF aerobatic team. For the Farnborough air show that year, they were joined by the first Gnat team – the Yellowjacks of No 4 FTS.

The start of an era

In 1964, it was planned to include in the SBAC Show at Farnborough an hour-long RAF contribution. In addition to the Red Pelicans of the Central Flying School, therefore, it was decided to form a second formation aerobatics team within RAF Flying Training Command. This team was based at No 4 Flying Training School at Valley on the Isle of Anglesey and consisted of five Hawker Siddeley Gnats, flying as "The Yellowjacks" under the leadership of Flight Lieutenant Lee Jones. This team was effectively the embryo of the Red Arrows.

The No 4 FTS team owed its formation almost solely to the personal initiative and enthusiasm of Lee Jones. Then 36, he was a very experienced fighter pilot who had recently begun instructing. His whole Service background was typical of the kind of background from which most RAF formation aerobatics pilots seem to emerge.

Lee, Liverpool-born, joined the RAF in October 1946. His first posting after flying training was to a Mosquito night fighter squadron. He went on to Meteor jets in 1952 and over the next five years gained experience of a mixed bag of jet fighters—F-84s, Sabres, Vampires, Venoms and Meteors as a pilot attack instructor at Sylt, Sabres and Hunters as a flight commander of No 112 Squadron at Bruggen.

His first taste of leading an aerobatic team was at the head of the formation put up by the Fighter Command Operational Conversion Unit at RAF Chivenor in 1958-59, and in 1960 he became a member of the Black Arrows.

Lee took the CFS instructors' course in 1962 and was posted to Valley the following year.

At that time, the Hawker Siddeley Gnat had been in service with the RAF for about a year. The first Gnats had been delivered to CFS itself, which was charged with carrying out initial trials and preparing the new training syllabus. Valley—which had the job of carrying out the intensive Service flying trials and of training the instructors who were to use the aircraft—received the first production Gnats some eight months later, in October 1962.

The Gnat was very different in design, concept and performance from the aircraft previously used by RAF flying training schools. It had originally been conceived as a single-seat light fighter and was used in that capacity by the Indian and Finnish air forces. Though its role in the RAF was essentially advanced flying training, with only a secondary operational capability, the Gnat remained far more a two-seat fighter than the conventional idea of a two-seat trainer.

It is, for example, genuinely transonic in performance, with a maximum speed of Mach 1.15 (about 760 mph) in a shallow dive and about Mach 0.95 in level flight. It has a fighter's lightness and responsiveness to control—in fact, it is true to say that it is lighter to handle and more sensitive than any front-line fighter either before or since. And the sophistication of its systems and equipment was certainly far in advance of anything the training schools had known up to that time.

To skilled and experienced instructors with a fighter-pilot background, the Gnat came as a welcome and refreshing development in the equipment used for the advanced flying phase of instruction. It would have been surprising if Lee Jones—with his enthusiasm for formation aerobatics already fired—had not itched for an opportunity to exploit the speed, exceptional manoeuvrability and precision of this lively newcomer in the aerobatics role.

The formation of the Yellowjacks (the name was originally simply a call-sign) was very much his personal achievement: he conceived the idea, put it forward, and was instrumental in getting it accepted.

Looking back at this distance of time, it may seem odd that there should ever have been doubts about the "rightness" of the Gnat for the aerobatic role. Remember, though, that the aircraft then was very new to service and, like almost every new aircraft, it had its share of teething troubles; when a new aircraft represents as big an advance over its predecessors as the Gnat did, personnel as well as equipment frequently need a "shakedown" period.

It was perhaps indicative of the misgivings about the serviceability standard which could be maintained with the aircraft in the initial stages that the No 4 FTS team was given a *ten-aircraft* establishment with which to maintain a *five-aircraft* formation.

Time, has put those early misgivings into proper perspective: the ten-aircraft establishment has never been increased for the Red Arrows, and they have not only constantly flown nine-aircraft formations but have taken part in hundreds more shows—often overseas and far from base—than were ever envisaged when the Yellowjacks were formed.

From many points of view, there was a "rightness" about the Gnat from the very start. For one thing, it is a good-looking aircraft, and that is not as unimportant in the context of formation aerobatics as some might think. More important, it had the handiness and accuracy of control which make possible slick changes of formation and the precision of flying so essential for display work when the aircraft must operate fairly near the ground at relatively high speeds. All this, plus unsurpassed swept-wing manoeuvrability, made the Gnat the ideal compromise between the powerful fighters of earlier years and the slower, less sprightly trainers which had temporarily filled the gap.

The success of the Yellowjacks brought this home, and official recognition of the fact soon followed. In 1965, the ten Gnats were formally established as the full-time RAF aerobatic team, operating under the immediate command of the CFS.

The "Red Arrows era" had begun.

The name itself was officially chosen, unlike the titles of some earlier teams which began as purely unofficial nicknames in press reports and elsewhere. The title of the team from which the Gnats took over—the Red Pelicans—had entirely logical origins: the aircraft had a red paint-scheme and a pelican is depicted in the official crest of the CFS. When the new CFS team was formed, the red finish was retained for the aircraft to emphasise the continuity of CFS's aerobatic teams, and it was logical to make "red" part of the title. "Arrows" not only suited the plan-form of the Gnat but also gave a link with the most famous of recent RAF aerobatic teams, the Black Arrows.

Initially, the Red Arrows were based at Fairford in Gloucestershire. This deliberate separation of the team from the main CFS establishment at Little Rissington reflected official policy towards display aerobatics. There were to be no half-measures: the team's sole responsibility was to be formation aerobatic displays, with no other commitments to compromise the efficient discharge of this duty.

There could obviously have been no other choice for the first leader but Flight Lieutenant Lee Jones. He took with him to the CFS three other pilots from the Yellowjacks: Flight Lieutenant Gerry Ranscombe (flying No 4 in the new team), Flying Officer Peter Hay (No 5), and Flight Lieutenant Henry Prince (No 7).

The intention initially was to display a seven-aircraft formation, with a reserve who would fly solo displays.

Four new pilots joined the ex-Yellowjacks personnel, therefore. Flight Lieutenant Bryan Nice from the 1964 Red Pelicans became deputy leader and No 2 in the formation. Flight Lieutenant Bill Loverseed from CFS became No 6 and I joined as No 3, both of us having been members, at different times, of the College of Air Warfare's Meteor team at Manby.

The forerunners of the Red Arrows — the Yellow-jacks of No 4 FTS, led by Flight Lieutenant Lee Jones, who in 1965 became the first leader of the Red Arrows.

The only occasion on which all four of Europe's leading national aerobatic teams have been photographed in the air together. Taken at Coxyde, Belgium, it shows the Fouga Magisters of Belgium's Diables Rouges leading the Red Arrows (top of picture), the Fiat G91s of Italy's Frecce Tricolori (bottom), and the Magisters of La Patrouille de France (left). Tucked in behind the Belgian team are three Jet Provosts of a second RAF team, the Gemini.

Flight Lieutenant Eric Tilsley, who came from the Red Pelicans to become the eighth member of the original team, deserves special mention: Eric, who flew solos at the displays, was the only "full-time" reserve pilot the Red Arrows have ever had and the position lasted only for that first year!

A thorough job was made of setting up the team for its new "full-time" aerobatics role, although for the first four years it functioned on a year-to-year basis with personnel loaned or seconded from other units. A Team Manager, Squadron Leader Dick Storer, was appointed to take overall command of the unit, with responsibility for administration and for making detailed arrangements for the season's programme. He also acted as the team's commentator at air shows.

Later, when the Team Leader was in overall command, the Team Manager's function became a largely administrative one, but he continued to act as commentator and "ferry pilot" for the 10th Gnat. In many ways, the Team Manager has always been the most hard-worked member of the team.

An Engineering Officer was also appointed to take charge of the ground support teams, Flying Officer Bill Green being the first holder of the post. In 1967, the Arrows were given their own Team Adjutant, Flight Lieutenant Ron Dench – a post subsequently held by Warrant Officer Leonard Ludlow. Then in 1969 the team was established on a permanent basis as the equivalent of a standard RAF squadron.

The Red Arrows' first public appearance was in May 1965 at the Biggin Hill International Air Fair. Success was immediate and 60 shows, including some in France and Belgium, were flown in that first season.

An indication of the impact made by the team can be gained from the fact that in March 1966 they were honoured with the Royal Aero Club's major award, the Britannia Trophy.

In the 1966 and 1967 seasons, when I had taken over the leadership from Lee Jones, the number of shows in which we took part rose to between 80 and 90. In most ways, though, our vintage year was 1968—the RAF's 50th anniversary year—when we gave no less than 98 displays. We should undoubtedly have topped 100 but for the cancellation of some overseas shows.

In a year like that, it is estimated that something like $2\frac{1}{4}$ million people see the Red Arrows "in the flesh". Even that figure shrinks, however, in comparison with the numbers who see the team on television through live and recorded coverage of shows like Farnborough and Biggin Hill.

Competition between the leading teams at international shows is friendly but fierce. Obviously there can be no absolute table of merit in so subjective an affair as formation aerobatics; personal tastes and preferences must make themselves felt and, since no two teams' performances are ever identical in content or style, some spectators will prefer one, some another.

Obviously, the factor which mainly dictates the nature of an aerobatic display is the type of aircraft being flown.

Every team tries to show off its aircraft to advantage. A team flying light and handy trainers like the Gnat or the French Fouga Magister cannot help but be different from, say, a team flying larger, more powerful combat aircraft like the American F-100 or McDonnell Phantom.

Many followers of formation aerobatics, however, feel that the performances of the various teams reflect differences in national character which go beyond the differences in the actual equipment they fly. They may be right. A lot of the "blood-and-thunder" style of outstanding American teams like the Thunderbirds and Blue Angels undoubtedly derives from plentiful use of reheat, but it is understandable if spectators also see in it a typically American love of power and speed.

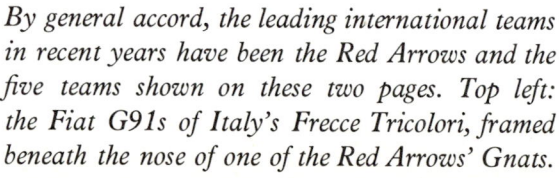

By general accord, the leading international teams in recent years have been the Red Arrows and the five teams shown on these two pages. Top left: the Fiat G91s of Italy's Frecce Tricolori, framed beneath the nose of one of the Red Arrows' Gnats. Below left: eleven Fouga Magisters of La Patrouille de France, in line astern and trailing smoke, at Farnborough in 1972. Right: the Grumman F-11 jets of the US Navy's Blue Angels displaying at the 1967 Paris Air Show.

In the same way, it is easy to see a typically Latin exuberance in the dashing displays of Italy's Frecce Tricolori and a touch of French elegance and *panache* about La Patrouille de France. With a bit of imagination and ingenuity, one could probably assign national characteristics to other teams like Belgium's Diables Rouges (which, like the French team, flies Fouga Magisters) and the Swedish team with its SAAB 105 aircraft.

What they all have in common is a blend of superb flying skill and discipline. To shine in this kind of international company, an aerobatic team has to be very, very good indeed. The art of formation aerobatics has probably been brought to its highest peak of perfection by the European teams, and there is no doubt that, for sheer professionalism and consistency, many aficionados rate the Red Arrows the best in Europe. Perhaps more important, the international teams themselves seem to share that feeling.

To a greater degree than any previous or contemporary team, the Red Arrows mastered the problems of providing the spectators with a continuous, flowing spectacle. Too often, the highlights in other teams' displays were achieved only at the expense of intervals of empty sky while their aircraft re-positioned themselves. If there is anything in the idea that different teams reflect different aspects of national character, perhaps it is the British readiness to accept compromise that made the Arrows ready to sacrifice ideas for spectacular manoeuvres if they did not fit into the overall pattern of the display sequence.

Whatever the reason, the RAF aerobatic team has not only consistently maintained the crispness and accuracy of its flying despite the demands of its long season, but has also consistently presented performances which make their 17-minute spot in the programme an intricate aerial ballet.

Above: Les Diables Rouges, equipped with French Fouga Magister trainers, 'on the break' at the Biggin Hill Air Fair in 1968. Below: the 1961 Thunderbirds team of the United States Air Force at the top of a loop in their North American F-100 Super Sabres.

There are two types of spectators at international air shows — the general public, seeking only an enjoyable spectacle, and professional pilots alert to the finer points of flying. The crowd at Nicosia, shown with the Red Arrows pictured above them, typifies the enthusiastic public following today.

It isn't done with mirrors...

Most critical judges of the aerobatic teams' displays are the pilots of the rival teams. Members of the Red Arrows are seen intently following the performance of another international formation team. Above them, La Patrouille de France is shown in a typical 'bomb-burst'.

At any major air show, the spectators range in knowledgeability from a small, select bunch of professional pilots who are capable of judging the finer points of flying to families who come simply to enjoy a day out.

A modern air force carries out most of its allotted tasks out of sight of the public, often beyond the borders of its home country or at great heights where the aircraft are either unseen above cloud or at best revealed by a contrail. Air displays therefore provide the public with its only real point of contact with the Service and, for this reason, it has always been the policy not only of the Red Arrows but also of the RAF as a whole to plan displays to appeal to the public rather than to just a few connoisseurs of flying. All the same, aerobatic pilots are human enough to want also to impress their fellow-professionals. A really good display satisfies both groups.

One of the greatest compliments ever paid to an aerobatic formation team came from a Suffolk farm labourer who lived near a team's practice base. Nobody could convince him that there were nine *separate* machines up there: he insisted that there was just one aircraft and that cunningly controlled mirrors made it look like nine!

Perhaps his was an extreme reaction but the fact remains that a perfectly trained team *does* fly as though it was one big aircraft and not nine small ones. It is not done by mirrors or any other kind of trickery, though: it is done simply by developing human skill and teamwork to a fine pitch by careful training, long experience and intensive practice.

Red Arrows at sunset over the River Severn.

Every hour of good daylight flying weather is valuable during pre-season practice.

There is no particular mystery about the art of formation flying. If you take your car and try to keep formation with another—keeping station, say, exactly three feet behind it—you can do it by careful steering and judicious use of the accelerator, so long as the driver ahead of you drives smoothly and does not fool around with his steering wheel or accelerator. The same holds true basically in flying, but with the additional complication that the machines are travelling far faster and in three planes of movement instead of two.

The starting point of formation flying is two aircraft flying together. One pilot aligns his aircraft with the other and, providing the lead pilot flies smoothly, a basic formation is achieved. The formating pilot concentrates his reactions and energies on following the leader's movements, making his own aircraft as far as possible an extension of the lead machine. By adding other aircraft to this basic pair, on the wings and astern, the formation is gradually built up.

In the final analysis, there are only three basic formation positions: echelon, line abreast and line astern. However many aircraft are used, all formation patterns are permutations of these three.

Echelon is the first formation for the pilot to master. The easiest way to explain it is to go back to the fundamental two-aircraft formation in which, in echelon, No 2 flies on the leader's right and slightly behind him, but in the same vertical plane. (If he flies slightly above the leader in the same position, then it is a stepped-up echelon). Lateral position needs to be maintained with the minimum use of the aircraft's ailerons, and pilots should master the technique of holding echelon formation absolutely smoothly and steadily before progressing to the more difficult line-abreast formation. With line abreast, as with echelon, the first requirement is to practise in straight and level flight until accurate assessment of the spacing between the aircraft becomes almost instinctive and automatic. Only then can a pilot move on to more ambitious aerobatic manoeuvres.

In line astern, the third basic formation, the following aircraft flies with its nose just behind and below the tail of the machine ahead and its fin and rudder just in the jet efflux. With the Gnat, most newcomers need to learn to overcome a tendency to over-control on the tailplane when flying this formation, and it takes practice to develop the judgment of trim manipulation and the anticipation needed to avoid this error. As a general rule, it is advisable in all formation positions to keep a slightly nose-down force as this helps to damp out any harsh longitudinal stick movements.

It does not matter what position a pilot is going to fly in the formation, all have to master these three basic formations. As more aircraft are added and different permutations of the three are built up, spacings between aircraft will vary. Maintaining evenly balanced spacing throughout the formation—whatever the number of aircraft involved and whatever the attitude in which they are flying—is the first essential for good displays.

Keeping station and distance accurately means that each pilot must have clearly defined reference points by which he can line up his machine with the next man's. It is a simple matter when only two aircraft are involved. With two Gnats in echelon, for instance, the pilot in No 2 will keep station by taking two imaginary reference lines on the leader's aircraft. One is a line through the triangle of the ejector-seat warning sign, just behind No 1's cockpit, and the navigation light on No 1's starboard wing-tip. The second is a line from the rear tip of the tail plane to the end of the jet pipe on No 1's aircraft. As long as No 2 keeps these two sets of references lined up, a perfect echelon formation will be held by the two Gnats.

Unvarying accuracy of station-keeping is the foundation stone on which all successful aerobatic formations are built — however large or small the formation, whatever manoeuvres are performed.

As the formation patterns grow larger and more complex, the task becomes more difficult. The leader's aircraft remains the principal reference point for every man in the formation but pilots in some positions need additional cross-references in order to hold station precisely.

It is easiest to illustrate this by reference to the "Diamond 9" formation, the most compact and most basic formation that can be flown by nine aircraft. "Diamond 9" has two aircraft in echelon on each side of the leader, Nos 2 and 4 being on his right and Nos 3 and 5 on his left. Nos 6 and 7 fly in line astern on the leader, No 8 in line astern on No 2, and No 9 in line astern on No 3. The only way in which the pilots in the outside and rearmost positions can maintain constant steadiness of spacing in formation is by continual reference to the leader while at the same time continuing to cross-refer to the aircraft beside or in front of them, ignoring any unnecessary movements by these inboard aircraft.

This art of station-keeping is essential for good formation display flying and is something which comes only with practice and experience. To aerobatic pilots, this is known as the "finesse technique", and it can be developed only by working as a team.

The reason why this skill has to be acquired, even by expert individual pilots, through sheer hard work with the team really comes down to a fact of human nature. Put two identical aircraft together, manned by pilots of identical skill, ask them to carry out a manoeuvre in unison—and, however well-matched the men and machines, there will always be some shifts in the position of one aircraft in relation to the other.
For one thing, the air is not a constant medium; there are all sorts of variations over very small distances. If the leader's position shifts, the pilot of the second aircraft has to try to anticipate it and compensate for it almost instantaneously.

Facing page: the camera freezes two Gnats on the downswing of a loop to create a photograph which captures some of the poetry of flight.

Photographer and photographed—Arthur Gibson took this shot of himself in the cockpit of a Gnat during a sortie with the Red Arrows. The team is shown above him, looping in 'Big Arrow' formation.

The Arrows above their home base at Kemble in 'Concorde' formation—a 'topical' formation suggested by the plan-form of the Anglo-French supersonic airliner based at nearby Fairford.

Accurate station-keeping and crisp, positive initiation of formation changes are the foundations on which the Red Arrows' displays are built. Use of smoke helps to define the formation patterns more clearly for the spectators.

When other aircraft are added to the formation, the farther they are from the origin of the shift in position, the more they will tend to enlarge the relative movement, increasing the demand on the skill of the pilot in accepting and compensating for it. When you are flying at 350/450 mph with only a few feet between your wingtip and the next man's, it is not human nature to accept these changes in relative position without some reaction. If your partner's aircraft edges towards you, your natural instinct is to edge away. If you do, though, you are apt to increase the amount of movement. Carry that effect cumulatively through a formation of nine aircraft, and the ninth man is apt to be reacting fairly violently—"flashing about", in fact.

The formation leader's first job, therefore, is to fly every manoeuvre as smoothly and accurately as possible. He has also to position the manoeuvres accurately within the confines of his display site and in such a way that they will be seen to the best advantage by the spectators. The more smoothly and steadily the leader flies, the easier the task of the rest of the team.

Obviously, if there is any shift or irregularity in the leader's flying, the sooner it is damped out within the formation the better; the farther it travels, the more it will be amplified. For that reason, it is normal practice to have the most experienced pilots in the positions immediately to the left and right and astern of the leader. If all three fly smoothly and steadily, there is a solid foundation on which the rest of the formation can be built.

Accurate station-keeping is achieved solely by "eye-ball" judgment on the part of the pilots—instruments cannot help them. "Finesse" depends very largely on building up confidence between all the members of the team and especially between the team and its leader. Without that confidence, it would be impossible to relax while in formation, and this is essential because tension leads to over-controlling and fatigue, especially in turbulent conditions.

On this point of relaxed flying, there is a favourite story among aerobatic pilots of a

On these pages, four typical formation manoeuvres are captured by the camera from different viewpoints. Above: a shot from inside the formation, with the photographer flying with the team's No 2, showing the Gnats on the downswing of a 'Diamond 9' loop.

Top: standing off the formation in a tenth aircraft, the photographer records two immaculate examples of formation flying by the Red Arrows. On left, the Gnats on the upswing of a loop in 'Big 9'; on right, the 'Apollo' formation suggested by the American spacecraft. Below, the camera aircraft follows the front four Gnats into Farnborough as they start the 'Twizzle'.

new man who, on joining the team, goes off for a work-out with the team leader.

After 15 minutes of continuous aerobatics, Red leader calls up his team-mate and says: "OK, 2, open up and relax".

Some moments later, he looks across and finds No 2 as close as ever and staring fixedly at him. So he repeats: "Open up, 2. Relax".

No 2 replies: "I am opened up and relaxed".

Red leader comes back: "All right, then. Tense up again, and I'll open up and relax".

All the leader can do is make sure that he provides as steady a reference point for his team as possible; he has to rely on them to keep station accurately. His task, in fact, is to concentrate literally on flying the whole team as one machine. For him, it feels very similar to flying a large, cumbersome aircraft through fighter-type manoeuvres.

Like the other pilots, the leader must rely on "eye-ball" judgment for the accuracy of his flying. Instruments are used solely to achieve the desired aerobatic entry and exit speeds and to maintain the planned sequence pattern. Even then, the leader will refer only momentarily to his airspeed indicator, altimeter and engine power instruments.

It may be thought that no experienced pilot should have much difficulty in simply flying smoothly, but it should be remembered that much of the interest in a display comes from quick changes of direction and manoeuvres which involve high g-loadings. A leader therefore has to develop the ability to compromise between the conflicting requirements of smooth flying and positive, crisp initiation of manoeuvres and changes of direction.

In more technical terms, one of the results is that experience shows that it is better for a leader to maintain positive g throughout the display sequence; the fewer relaxations he makes, the easier it is for the team to follow his manoeuvres. The rate at which g is applied can be crucial because a tendency to snatch or apply g abruptly can take the team unawares, causing raggedness.

Pilots new to leading a formation are apt to be too gentle in the rate of application, though, and this leads to a lack of crispness in manoeuvres which tends to dull the overall performance.

Naturally, the optimum amount of g varies from one type of aircraft to another and from one kind of manoeuvre to another. With the Gnat as flown by the Red Arrows, the ideal g loadings for loops are between $3\frac{1}{2}$ and $4g$, with a top limit of about $4\frac{1}{2}g$, and for rolls between 2 and $2\frac{1}{2}g$.

When one talks of formation aerobatic "manoeuvres", most ordinary spectators probably think that there is an almost endless variety. In fact, just as the different formations are built up from the three basics of echelon, line abreast and line astern, so all manoeuvres are really variations and combinations of three "fundamentals": loop, roll and wing-over. The loop must be the oldest of all aerobatic manoeuvres. It needs to be very precisely flown and smoothly executed if it is to be effective in formation. Initiation of the loop has to be progressive but positive, and the right degree of smoothness of entry into the manoeuvre is more easily achieved from a shallow dive than from straight and level flight. The leader's aim should be to reach maximum g loading when 40 or 50 degrees of the loop have been completed, and back pressure should be maintained to hold just clear of the pre-stall "nibble".

At the top of the loop, it is generally necessary to ease off the back pressure, but it needs to be increased again as the formation enters the second half of the loop, with the leader aiming at a constant pull for final recovery in order to flow into the next manoeuvre in the sequence.

The technique for a formation barrel roll is governed partly by the size and frontal "spread" of the formation. Three or four compactly grouped aircraft can be rolled quite quickly without much back pressure being applied. A larger and "wider-fronted" formation has to take it rather more slowly, with a definite back pressure being maintained throughout the manoeuvre (with Gnats, about $2-2\frac{1}{2}g$). There is an instinctive inclination to ease off the pressure when inverted at 2,000-3,000 ft but, if the leader

The Red Arrows in 'Diamond 9' formation over the Kent cliffs during a photographic sortie from Manston airfield.

gives way to this temptation, the wing-men will tend to be thrown or the whole formation appear "dished".

The wing-over, the third of the basic manoeuvres, is a combination of a loop and a turn. If the leader does not fly it correctly, he can make life difficult for his team. Again, the most important thing for the leader to do is to avoid abrupt variations of control force; once he has set the angle of bank and pull force, he needs to keep them constant.

By judiciously juggling various permutations of the three basic formations and the three basic manoeuvres, an aerobatic team can build up a surprisingly varied display routine. However well each component formation and manoeuvre are flown, though, they will all be wasted if the whole display sequence is not presented in a manner which shows them to the best advantage and continuously maintains interest.

This really comes down to the leader having his team in the right place, with the right formation, at the right time. It sounds simple, but it is in some ways the most difficult piece of technique for a new leader to master.

A number of factors need to be taken into account when it comes to this elusive question of "presentation" but the over-riding one should always be to ensure the the public spectator can see all that is going on. Almost the first thing to determine is the datum point for the display. This is dictated mainly by the crowd line at the particular show. At many air shows such as Paris or Farnborough, datum will almost certainly be a point opposite the President's tent, on a line running parallel to the crowd line.

The leader's objective is to start and end each manoeuvre, or to time the highlight of it, so that it occurs exactly on the datum line. A perfectly executed formation loop, for instance, will begin and end on the datum line. The ultimate, in fact, is to present the whole sequence so that no spectator needs to turn his head more than 60 degrees to either side or raise it more than 50 degrees.

A photograph which conveys something of the tightness and precision of the Arrows' formation flying: the team rolling in 'Wineglass' formation.

The attractive lines of the Gnat—one of the many qualities which make it a superb formation aerobatics aircraft—can be clearly seen as the team flies over wooded country.

In a perfectly executed loop, the manoeuvre will begin and end on the datum line and—on windless days—the team will fly through its own smoke trail at the bottom of the loop.

In loops, the aim is to have the team either running straight at datum point or flying directly away from it, and the datum remains the focus of the whole manoeuvre whether it is carried out at a relatively fine angle to the datum line or a relatively large one. In rolling manoeuvres, the best presentation is achieved by running parallel to the crowd, timing the roll so that the aircraft cross the datum line inverted.

Weather conditions obviously have a very big bearing on presentation. The Red Arrows have always aimed to have three basic display sequences, tailored to conditions ranging from good to just short of non-flyable.
It is the leader's decision as to which of the three shall be used. Within these three basic "frameworks", however, he may also decide upon a number of minor variations in presentation. For instance, if marginal cloud conditions limit the height available, it pays to reduce the frontage of a wide formation so that a faster, flatter roll can be flown.

The biggest test of a team's experience and resourcefulness is likely to be provided on overseas tours. It is not unusual for the team to go into a display without previously having flown at that particular venue and without opportunity for previous practice "on site". The leader then has to draw on his experience to "feel it out" as he and the team begin the display. To get the positioning and timing of the various manoeuvres right, he may have to be harsher than usual with control movements, tightening loops and turns. The team learns to accept this and, with experience, can often anticipate what the leader will want of them.

A typical instance of this occurred on a tour the Red Arrows did to the French Riviera. Our first display was at Monte Carlo.
We had been there before but the weather turned foul and, to give a display at all, we had to give an unusually flat "flattie", as the bad-weather display is sometimes called.

Next day the weather was brilliant. We had two display dates, one at Cannes and one at Nice. We had not been to Cannes before and there was no chance of practice. In one way,

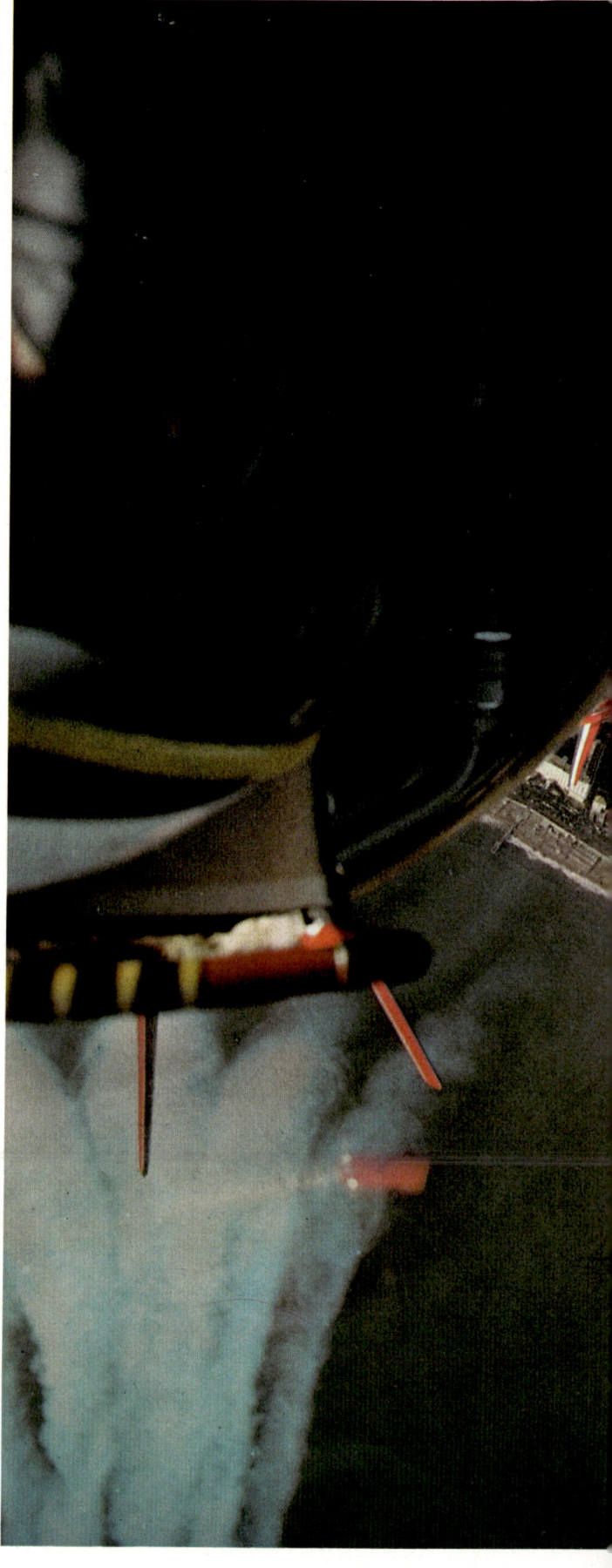

Informal get-together between the 1969 'synchro pair' in the team's hotel before displays at Cannes and Nice. The 'synchro' leader, Terry Kingsley (No 6) is on right, and Ian Dick (No 7) on left.

Two moments from the Red Arrows' 1969 visit to the French Riviera. Left, the Gnats inverted at the top of a loop over the harbour and sea-front at Cannes. Right, sunset run-in for the show the same evening for crowds lining the famous Promenade des Anglais at Nice.

there were no problems because we were flying over the sea and displaying to crowds lining the harbour and sea-front. As we were positioning before starting the display sequence, Terry Kingsley—then leading the synchro pair—and I had to decide the best way of presenting synchro sequences.
I asked Terry if he thought that he and Ian Dick, his partner, could keep within the confines of the harbour itself.
Terry reckoned they could—and it turned out to be one of the best synchro performances of the season.

The same qualities of anticipation and swift but calculating assessment of the situation are needed all through the display season. Anticipation plays a big part in carrying out formation changes in mid-manoeuvre in such a manner that they look slick and crisp but not rushed to the ground spectator. A good deal of the continuity of interest in a display depends upon a succession of smooth changes of formation, to which the spectators' attention is usually drawn by the team's commentator. Safety—always a top priority in display flying—as well as crispness and evenness of formation changes demands that no move should be made without a clear-cut, readily understandable order from the leader. It does not take long, though, for each pilot to learn to think a move ahead so that he is ready for each order even before he is given his cue.

A good many different qualities help to make up a successful formation aerobatics pilot but anticipation and alertness are certainly among the most important of them.
Without these qualities in every pilot, there must be a time-lag between the giving of an order and the completion of the action it calls for. It is the elimination of those tiny delay and hesitancies which gives the Red Arrows' displays the assured and polished professionalism which, since their first season, has made them perhaps the most consistently successful of all international teams.

Terry Kingsley leads his 'synchro pair' partner over the West Country landscape during an early-season practice sortie.

A matter of polish

The ultimate difference between an aerobatic team of average competence and an outstanding one is often a matter of polish—and in formation aerobatics polish is something that comes only as the result of hard work by every member of the team.

Without question, the decision to establish the Red Arrows on a "permanent" basis as the RAF aerobatic team has made it a lot easier to achieve that final, all-important finish. Although the team is part of the Central Flying School—which has been described as "the centre of pure flying within the RAF"—the Arrows operate as a detached unit (the equivalent of a standard RAF squadron) from their own base at Kemble in Gloucestershire.

Normal complement of the team consists of the leader plus eight pilots, a team manager (also a pilot), an engineering officer, an adjutant and 40 to 60 NCO and airmen ground crew. Each year, about three pilots are posted from the team to other jobs in the RAF, so that a typical tour of duty with the Red Arrows is about three years.

New pilots usually arrive at Kemble in the early autumn, as the display season is coming to an end. Their first task, as a rule, is to re-familiarise themselves with the Gnat, which many of them will not have flown for some time. Then they will start carrying out some preliminary formation training practice.

While this is going on, the rest of the team split up for their annual leave. When they return, there is always a stack of paperwork to catch up on, while the engineering officer and his men have to carry through a complete overhaul programme on the ten Gnats and make any necessary modifications.

The complete team—ground crew as well as aircrew—reassembles in early January, and it is then that the hard grind of training really begins.

If a new leader is appointed, it is particularly important that he should overlap with his predecessor so that the new man can benefit from his experience and his knowledge of the members of the team. Every new leader of the Red Arrows has a lot to learn about the rudiments of the job—both from the display point of view and from the organisational aspect—and it is a lot easier to do if he can "sit in" with the departing leader over the latter part of the season.

The balance between smoothness of flying and tightness of presentation which distinguishes the really first-class aerobatic formations can only be achieved if the leader has developed a special "feel" for display flying. It is also a quality which soon gets rusty if it is not used. A new leader of the Red Arrows will concentrate initially on cultivating this almost instinctive "feel" and sense of judgment through intensive solo practice. He will practise low-level aerobatics, working to a selected datum point on the ground and within the kind of limits which he can expect at air shows.

He must learn to gauge the points at which to pull up into a loop, roll or wing-over. He must master the technique of manoeuvring at constant rates. He must sharpen his judgment of the effects of wind and weather and develop the ability to make automatic allowance for them during a display.
He must work out and commit to memory the speeds and power settings essential to carry out all the manoeuvres and set-pieces smoothly and precisely.

At the same time, he must get to know all his pilots, building up mutual confidence between himself and them and between all the individuals in the team. He will start formation training by leading small formations—using the most experienced members of the team—in basic manoeuvres.

By this time, the new pilots will have become accustomed to flying the Gnat at the low altitudes typical of display work and have brushed up at safe heights on the three basic formations—echelon, line abreast and line astern.

A typical scene at the Red Arrows' home base at RAF Kemble, Gloucestershire, during the early months of the year as the team work up their season's display sequence.

The first phase of full team training aims at familiarising each man with his place in the formation which, once settled, he will retain throughout the season. Each position calls for slight variations in technique so that every pilot has to develop a special "feel" for his slot.

To a watching crowd, for instance, all the aircraft in a formation appear to be flying at the same speed. But in some manoeuvres —particularly turns—wide differences occur, and the man on the outside of a turn has farther to fly to keep station and must therefore fly faster. During certain pattern changes, hardly two throttles in the team will be at the same setting.

As the new pilots gain experience, more aircraft are added to the small formations with which the leader started, until full strength is achieved. Most training is carried out at Kemble. The English weather being what it is, however—especially in the early months of the year—good flying conditions have to be exploited to the full, and this may mean sometimes switching to other airfields to take advantage of better weather in another area. Weather permitting, the team will fly up to four sorties a day during training.

Once the full-strength team has acquired confident mastery over loops, rolls and wing-overs at a safe height, practices are flown at lower altitudes. Too much practice at relatively high levels and in smooth air is unwise. All aircraft handle differently at the low altitudes characteristic of display flying, and pilots need to get used to flying close to the ground and in turbulent conditions as soon as possible.

Once leader and team have reached the level of proficiency needed for them to be authorised down to lower altitudes, the team leader can start to shift the emphasis to the actual content and composition of the season's display sequences. This is an exercise in collective "creative imagination" by all the pilots!

Squadron Leader Ray Hanna and members of the 1970 season during a briefing session at Kemble. Seated on extreme right is the 1971 leader, Squadron Leader Dennis Hazell.

The Red Arrows have made a feature of splitting their nine-ship formations, in mid-sequence, into a seven-Gnat section and a 'synchro pair'. Alternation of the pair's manoeuvres with those of the seven-ship formation—seen above in a '7-Arrow' loop—helps to give their displays their characteristic continuity and flow and maintain interest from start to end of the sequence.

Careful synchronisation of the two sections' manoeuvres is essential for a smooth-flowing display. Ultimate responsibility for presentation rests with the Team Leader, and Ray Hanna is seen above (standing), casting a critical eye over one of the 'synchro pair's' manoeuvres.

The composition of a Red Arrows display sequence, in fact, is essentially a team effort and the product of a good deal of thought and experiment. Over the years, of course, the Arrows have built a basic repertoire of formation patterns and manoeuvres, some of which are very much identified with the team. The formation "twinkle roll" is an example of this; the "Concorde" formation, introduced as a tribute to the supersonic airliner, is another.

Each year, though, every aerobatic team tries to introduce something new. Competition between the international teams is keen and air-display crowds—like all "show-business" audiences—have an appetite for novelty.

As time goes on, it gets more and more difficult to think up really new and different manoeuvres or formations. With only three basic formations and only three basic manoeuvres, there is a limit to the number of permutations anybody can produce.

There are also limits to the innovations possible with any one type of aircraft. This is partly a matter of aircraft performance, which is not really going to change after the type is established in service, and partly a matter of what might be called "aesthetics".

This may sound rather fanciful, but the fact is that formations which look attractive when flown by swept-wing aircraft such as the Gnat do not always work nearly as well for straight-wing types like the Fouga Magister, and vice-versa. By and large, the best formation patterns are those which echo the shape of the individual aircraft composing them; the lines of the overall pattern are sharper and more clearly defined because they duplicate and enlarge the lines of the aircraft themselves.

This means that the Gnat, with wings swept back at nearly 45 degrees, is best suited by patterns which are also "swept back" so that the spectator watching from the ground can draw an imaginary straight line along the wing leading edges of the outermost aircraft.

There is a bit more to it, though, than "aesthetic considerations". In part, it comes back to the old aviation saying: "What looks right is right". Formations which are not aesthetically attractive are generally the most difficult to fly perfectly. For instance, it is more difficult to hold a really immaculate line abreast in swept-wing aircraft like the Gnat than in a straight-wing type. The Gnat pilot has no natural reference point to help him line up on his neighbour, whereas the pilot of a Magister, for instance, has an ideal reference in the tip of the straight wing.

All the same, no team can really afford to veto all these "less suitable" formations when there are basically only three formations to play with. So, to add variety, the Red Arrows have included in their display sequences formations based on line-abreast, such a "Leader's Benefit" (with the leader flying just ahead of the rest of the formation, in line abreast on either side of his aircraft); "Kings Cross" (a combination of line abreast and line astern); and "Tee" (line abreast and line astern forming the shape of the letter T).

There is a secondary consideration which applies to these "unsuitable" formations: pilots in the team know that the "professional element" in the crowd will appreciate the extra degree of skill involved in flying them really accurately, so there is a certain extra satisfaction in flying them.

The dominant consideration in planning a display sequence, though, remains the need to satisfy the ordinary *public* spectator. Plenty of formations and manoeuvres might give special enjoyment or particular satisfaction to the pilots but just will not mean anything to the man on the ground. If they are not crowd-pleasers, they will not qualify for inclusion in the Arrows' display. Nor will any manoeuvre which might impose undue risk under display conditions.

In a sense, the public spectator is present at every practice sortie flown by the Red Arrows. As a rule, his representative is the Team Manager. Stopwatch in hand, he can be seen out on the airfield, timing every manoeuvre and assessing it from the viewpoint of the man in the crowd.

Every training sortie is also filmed by the team's cine cameraman, and the film record and Team Manager's comments provide an objective record during the team de-briefings, at which every aspect of the sortie is analysed and discussed. A really *good* de-brief after a really *bad* trip, in fact, would make quite a book in itself!

For every hour spent in the air, two or three are spent in de-briefing and discussion on the ground. Imperfections are pin-pointed, criticisms of individual performance are aired, ways of improving presentation are thrashed out. Gradually, a display sequence is built up which will live up to the standards of continuous, flowing action and interest which the Red Arrows have set themselves from the start.

Careful planning, a good deal of ingenuity, a lot of hard work—they all play their part. It is one thing to devise a particular manoeuvre which looks great on its own; it is quite another thing to fit it into a series of interlinked manoeuvres so that they flow into and out of each other and keep the interest going without a break.

"Bomb bursts", for instance, are popular and spectacular features of aerobatic displays. It takes careful planning, however, to fit them satisfactorily into a sequence, since it is in the nature of this manoeuvre that the aircraft should end up scattered to the four points of the compass. Unless the manoeuvre is used as the finale to a display, therefore, some method has to be found to retain the spectators' interest while the aircraft join up again for the next manoeuvre—even jet aircraft as handy and manoeuvrable as the Gnat need a fair amount of space and time in which to do that.

Flat "bomb bursts" are popular with the members of a team; the bottom of the manoeuvre affords them a few seconds of individual freedom and a rare opportunity for authorised "wiring"—the aerobatic pilot's term for low flying.

In formation aerobatic display flying, there is constant pressure for innovation and change, and the 'Concorde' formation illustrated on page 37 evolved into 'Super Concorde', shown opposite.

This is why the idea of splitting the team into two sections at some points in the display has proved so useful. Some teams use a solo aircraft to fill in while the main formation is "off-stage", some larger formations split into two more or less equal sections. The Red Arrows have used both methods, but perhaps their speciality has been the use of two Gnats in a synchronised "double act".

Normally, the two synchro pilots will be chosen from men who have had at least one full season in the team. Whenever possible, each man will fly one year as No 2 in the pair and take over as the synchro leader the following season. The two men chosen have to put in an extra training stint in order to work up their own double act while also taking part in full team training.

When the full display sequence has been worked out, close attention is given to synchronising the manoeuvres of this pair of aircraft with those of the main formation. Split-second timing is essential. With really tight timing, it is possible not only to maintain the flow of interest while the main formation is "off-stage" but also to step up the pace of the whole performance quite dramatically and inject extra excitement.

The mental and physical strain of flying three or four training sorties a day, especially in the turbulent conditions likely to be encountered at low level, is considerable. Depending on their position in the formation, pilots may be pulling up to $4\frac{1}{2}$g in loops and other manoeuvres, and a full day's flying of this kind takes its toll of even the fittest. At the end of it, everybody is glad to relax in the crew room.

The Arrows' display season normally opens in April or May, by which time the full display sequence and its poor-weather alternatives have not only been perfected in practice but also seen by the Commander-in-Chief, Training Command, whose approval is necessary before the team can display in public. From then on, it is rare for changes

Left, the team looping in 'Big Arrow'. Right, four Gnats photographed inverted at the top of a loop in mathematically precise line-abreast.

to be made in the sequence. Refinements and modifications will certainly be considered at any time in the season. New ideas which survive critical discussion in the crew room may eventually be incorporated, but they have to be strokes of near-genius if they are capable of being fitted into the routine so carefully planned and rehearsed during the months of constant practice.

With the Red Arrows, it is a matter of pride that only the very worst weather will prevent them meeting a display commitment. Weather minima for the full display sequence are a cloud base of 4,000 ft and visibility of $1\frac{1}{2}$-2 nautical miles. In essence, this show consists of a series of loops, rolls and wing-overs which take full advantage of good conditions to demonstrate the more elaborate set-piece manoeuvres worked out in the closed season.

Second choice is the intermediate or "rolling" display, which requires a minimum cloud base of 2,000 ft and consists basically of rolling manoeuvres which do not depend on height for effect.

In really poor weather, with the cloud base down to 700 ft and visibility only 1-$1\frac{1}{2}$ miles, the show still goes on, but it will be a "flat" display. Basically this comprises level turns demonstrating the various formation patterns, plus some set-pieces and solo synchronised manoeuvres.

All three variations are worked out in detail before the season starts because the final decision as to which sequence is to be used may sometimes be taken only after the team is airborne. Every move in every sequence therefore has to be memorised by every pilot in the team.

The aim is to make sure that—from the moment the ground crews start the Orpheus engines at the season's first show to the moment when the Gnats sweep in for their final stream-landing of the year—the interest shall be continuous, the standard consistent, and the polish never less than 100 per cent professional.

The slower the speed, the greater the smoke. With undercarriages down, the team makes a low-level formation pass in 'Big Arrow' for the benefit of photographers at the press day which preceded the opening in the 1973 season.

At the heart of the Red Arrows' success is teamwork—but formation aerobatics are not the only field in which the key to successful teamwork is successful leadership.

A mixture of qualities is needed by an aerobatic team leader. Flying ability is only one of them—an essential one if the leader is to command the respect and confidence which are the keystones of successful teamwork. But there are plenty of superb pilots who still do not make successful team leaders, though they may well be highly successful as members of a team.

It is the leader's job to present the team and its display sequences to the best possible advantage, no matter what the difficulties. To do that consistently over a full season, with all its changes of display site and weather conditions, demands a special kind of flair. It is hard to say exactly what it is but, if it is not present in a pilot's make-up from the beginning, no amount of experience seems able to develop it.

When it comes to the actual flying, some of the pilots in other positions in the team have a tougher job than the leader. Certainly, anybody who listened into the R/T conversation during a display could be excused for thinking that there was not really very much to leading a team.

Radio contact is maintained every moment of the display, but there is an absolute minimum of "chat". The leader's commands have to be clear, completely unambiguous and very brief. Team members, for their part, normally do no more than acknowledge those orders which involve them personally in making a move to change the shape of a formation. Usually, all they do is call out the number of their particular position as they make the move.

A typical R/T conversation during a display could go like this:

Leader: Arrow—go.
Acknowledgments: Eight. Nine.
Leader: Rolling in . . . (no acknowledgment required). Smoke on—go . . . (again no acknowledgment needed). Tightening . . . rolling out . . . (no acknowledgment necessary) . . . Split—go.
Acknowledgment from synchro pair leader: Six clear.
Leader: Pulling up . . . power . . . Box—go.
Acknowledgment: Four in.
Synchro leader: Split—go.
Acknowledgment from 2nd synchro man: Seven.
Synchro leader: Thirty-two (32,000 ft altitude).
Leader: Vixen—go.
Acknowledgments: Four. Five.
Leader: Throttling back . . . smoke off—go.

Just to put it in perspective, that terse exchange of advisory and executive commands and acknowledgments would be all the R/T conversation to be heard in some $1\frac{1}{4}$ to $1\frac{1}{2}$ minutes of flying, during which the formation would change four times. Obviously, it would be impossible to go through a complicated display sequence with commands cut down to such bare essentials if the team has not practised to the point where every pilot has a clear picture of the overall sequence and can react almost instinctively to each order. In a sense, the leader uses commands rather the way the conductor of an orchestra uses his baton: to control timing and bring each man in "on cue". Every command, as you will have noticed, is prefaced by an advisory word or two, so that each pilot has the necessary fraction of time to set himself for his next control movement: Vixen. (A pause). Go.

R/T conversation needs particularly careful timing once the synchro pair (Nos 6 and 7 in the formation) have broken away. They need to keep close radio contact with each other and with the formation, while the leader still has to lead the main formation. At no stage in the performance, though, is there room for hesitancy or "chat".

Playing to the camera: one of the team makes a low-level pass especially for the benefit of the cameraman during the making of Arthur Gibson's film, 'The Red Arrows'.

It has to be remembered, of course, that no RAF pilot comes to formation aerobatics without earlier experience both of aerobatics and of formation flying: they are both essential elements in the training of Service pilots and particularly of fighter pilots. Display flying is a logical development of skills which the pilots acquire early in their Service careers. It is the leader's task to harness those skills and make sure that they are presented in such a way that they can be appreciated by crowds who probably know little of the finer points of flying.

Enthusiasm and a capacity for hard work are as important a part of a leader's make-up as sheer flying ability and experience. If a pilot does not have real enthusiasm for display flying, he is hardly likely to develop the flair which leading a team demands. He also needs the knack of getting the same qualities from all the pilots in the team.

It is scarcely necessary to say that he must possess the ability to command, and his authority within the team must be total. But no mere disciplinarian or martinet could maintain a team's collective enthusiasm and co-operation throughout a full display season.

Contrary to what some people think, the pilots of an aerobatic team are not prima donnas: it is not a job in which temperament can be tolerated. They are all *professionals*—which does not mean they are stereotypes. As anybody who has spent a few hours with any Red Arrows team will know, they are all highly individual "personalities". If they were nothing but automatons, stolidly carrying out orders, their displays would hardly have the dash and elan which characterise the leading international teams.

From the start of the display season until they split up to take their annual leave around the end of October, the Red Arrows are rarely in one place for long and members are rarely out of each other's company for more than a few hours. The flying makes demands which tax both physical and nervous stamina. Whenever possible, the Arrows try to depart for a display in the UK 24 hours in advance; overseas tours can mean that they are away from base for a week or so. Most air shows are held at weekends, so the team cannot look for weekends off. On top of it all is a lengthy round of social occasions which are more or less mandatory in view of the public relations aspect of the whole operation.

It is thus a somewhat introverted, inbred existence during the display season, and the team tends to be driven back on its own resources. The constant travelling—and travelling light, at that—means that the members live out of suitcases half the year. As one pilot said: "You can't start wearing new underwear without the rest of the team noticing—and probably pulling your leg about it".

With so much depending on unremitting concentration and speed of reaction, the whole delicate balance could easily be upset if there were personal friction between individuals. It is not overstating it to say that each man's life could depend on there being total confidence between all the team's members.

As leader, you know soon enough whether you have the confidence of the rest of the team, but they are not apt to say so in so many words. I was told, though, that one pilot, leaving after three years with the Red Arrows, summed up his attitude to the leader by saying: "Perhaps two, three times in a year I feel I'm taking my life in my hands and holding it out to him and saying: 'There you are, boss—it's yours'". (I am also told that the pilot in question covered up this rather uncharacteristic piece of sentiment with "Ah, don't mind me—it's probably the beer talking"—which sounds much more like him!)

Perhaps I would not have put it quite that way myself, and perhaps there was a degree of exaggeration in the "my-life-in-his-hands" idea, but I know from the days when I flew under Lee Jones that there are times when you know you are staking quite a lot on one man's judgment.

Yet, although this trust and confidence are most vital in the air, it is probably true to say that it is easier to maintain teamwork and discipline while flying than when on the ground. All the pilots, after all, are highly-trained, highly-experienced members of a highly-disciplined military force, and habits

The face of a leader: Squadron Leader Ian Dick, a member of the team from 1968 to 1970 and its leader in 1972 and 1973, ready for take-off in the cockpit of his Gnat.

built through years of training and service do not yield easily to spurts of temperament.

But on the ground, in the self-centred little world of the aerobatic teams, outlets have to be found to release the tensions of the day. Heavy-handed discipline would only increase the tensions, and the leader has to have the knack of maintaining the right balance between discipline and individual freedom without pulling rank—but with sufficient ruthlessness in reserve to make rank tell if there is no alternative.

The onus for picking men who will fit into the team rests with the leader. Usually, he will allow existing members a say in the choice of a new pilot, and any newcomer must be acceptable also to HQ, Central Flying School, HQ, Training Command, and the Ministry of Defence, but the final decision is the leader's. He cannot afford to pick a man who will not stand up to the stresses of the operation or who falls short, in any way, of the standards of "professionalism" it demands. If he does make a wrong choice, he has to have sufficient honesty and ruthlessness to recognise the fact and to discard the man as soon as it is clear that he will not make the grade.

Above, the ground spectator's view of the cross-over in the 'Roulette' manoeuvre and, right, the same moment seen from the cockpit of one of the 'synchro pair' aircraft taking part.

Three crew-room scenes at Kemble. Above left, team members find amusement in the scrapbook kept each year by the Red Arrows. Above right, every one of the flood of letters received from the general public is scrupulously answered by the team. Below, the 'trophy cabinets' provide a permanent home for gifts ranging from cuddly toys to valuable trophies and paintings.

There are always more volunteers for the Red Arrows than there are vacancies, and most of them—because the RAF is really a fairly small world—will be known to at least some of the pilots already in the team. Normally, there is little difficulty in assessing flying ability, and the reputation of most really good pilots tends to travel ahead of them. What the leader will chiefly be looking for is "compatibility"—the quality which will enable a new man to slot into the team quickly and congenially.

"Compatibility" where the Red Arrows are concerned has always included a sense of humour. Describing a Mediterranean tour with the team in *Flight International*, Bob Rodwell once wrote: "Even though expecting the rapport, the social integration of the team is an amazing thing to experience for any length of time.

"They are a consummate flying turn but could hold their own in high-priced cabaret, too. The repartee cannot be reported—all of it is too fast to note, and much of it unprintable anyway. All are witty in their different styles . . ."

Red Arrows humour does indeed tend to be irreverent, ribald, often bawdy. It tends to poke fun at pomposity and anything that smacks of unnecessary officialdom. And it does not take too seriously the "mystique" of aerobatic flying or the exaggerated regard some people show for the pilots engaged in it. One cannot imagine a humourless man lasting long in that kind of company.

Lee Jones perhaps helped to set the tone for this as for so many of the other aspects of the Arrows. His humour was very much in the mainstream of the Red Arrows style. Like all the other members of the team over the years, he found the idea of the Arrows being "daredevils of the air"—popular with some journalists—food for laughter.

Each year, the team keeps a scrapbook of press reports and articles. In one of the early books, there is a back cover of an RAF Germany air safety journal which illustrates the tongue-in-the-cheek attitude which Lee and most of the other pilots take towards their role. A photograph shows him in the cockpit of his Gnat, being interviewed by the British Forces' Broadcasting Service.

The caption has Lee saying:

". . . belt down the runway upside down, hanging from the cockpit edge by my bootcaps, and snatch the rose from behind the lady's ear. Sometimes I get the ear, too. I was specially selected, of course . . ."

Whoever wrote that caption has captured the Arrows' style well—especially with the mock-solemnity of the line, "I was specially selected, of course . . ."

Just in passing, it is worth mentioning that the joke in this instance was the sugar on a perfectly serious message about flight safety. As the journal pointed out: "The Red Arrows perform many feats for which they train, and *train* and TRAIN. Leave the death-defying to those who have *trained* to do it *safely*".

Those are sentiments which every pilot who has ever flown with the team would echo. There is no point in pretending that there is not always an element of risk in formation aerobatics. However skilled the pilots and however reliable their aircraft, there must always be a percentage of danger in flying at 350-400 mph at low levels, with a wing-tip separation of perhaps as little as four feet. But, if the environment contains danger, the professional does all he can to minimise it, not to increase it—and the Red Arrows are consummate professionals.

No pilot in the team takes risks that would place himself or his colleagues in jeopardy—and anybody who did would be out so fast he would not know what had hit him. Because they are professionals, all the members of the team recognise the risks and use their training and experience to contain them. They are no different in this respect from other similar professionals (such as motor-racing drivers) who pit themselves against an environment which is inherently dangerous. One of the main purposes of the protracted practising and rehearsal carried out by the team, of course, is to eliminate from the final display sequence any manoeuvres which might represent excessive risk under public display conditions.

Traditional prelude to each season is Press Day. In 1973, additional interest was provided by the 'unveiling' by Team Leader Ian Dick (left of easel in top picture) of Arthur Gibson's photographs of the Arrows in formation with Concorde (one of which is reproduced overleaf). Below, press photographers take shots of a slightly self-conscious line-up of members of the 1973 team.

There have been tragic incidents involving members of the Arrows, as everybody knows, but it helps to put them in perspective if it is remembered that they occurred *in practice* and not at any of the 600 or so public shows the team has given.

All the same, a streak of controlled aggressiveness is an essential characteristic in an aerobatic pilot; it drives him to hold an accurate position while in formation and to make formation changes quickly and positively.

Every member of the Red Arrows is, of course, a volunteer, but they are all volunteers from within a highly professional elite; amateurism, however inspired it may be, has no place in formation aerobatics or, indeed, in any kind of RAF flying operations.

No pilot is accepted for membership of the team with less than 1,000 hours' first-pilot experience. Ideally, this will include a background of fighter flying and preferably some low-level experience. Once in a while, perhaps, a pilot with a flair for formation aerobatics will emerge from a rather different background. At all events, it is useless for anybody to apply unless he has an "above average" pilot rating.

Because no pilot can stack up experience in that kind of depth in a hurry, the age level of the team tends to be higher than most outsiders expect. Perhaps that misconception has been encouraged by some newspapers' tendency to portray aerobatic pilots as dashing young daredevils, but generally the average age has been around 30.

To many pilots with a fighter background, formation aerobatics offer a kind of satisfaction which they get from no other kind of flying. Bill Loverseed—who was a founder-member of the Arrows in 1965, returned to the team in 1970, and became the leader the following year—was not speaking only for himself when he said: "Once you've done it at the top level, you feel it's the only sort of flying for you."

It is not the glamour of the job that appeals: that is over-rated—there is far more hard work and grinding routine than outsiders realise. The satisfaction comes from being able to apply all the skills you have spent years in acquiring before an appreciative audience. It comes from being part of a close-knit team with people who share the same skills and whose ability you respect. And, at the same time, it comes from flying in a way which gives you all a chance to express your own personality.

Most aircrew in the RAF recognise that the existence of a successful RAF aerobatic team is an asset to the Service and to Britain at large. Asked how he felt about the fuss made of the Arrows on one overseas tour, the captain of a supporting Argosy aircraft shrugged and said: "They're part of the RAF and so am I. I couldn't do their job but I'm not sure that they could do mine. As far as I'm concerned, we are all doing a job for the Service, and I'm glad to help them if it means that a lot of people are going to end up thinking better of the RAF than they did before."

You need both competitiveness and pride even to want to become an aerobatics pilot. In the RAF, becoming a member of the Red Arrows has for some years meant that you were at the top of a particular tree. Every member of the team, I think, takes pride not only in that but also in the fact that, as part of the team, he is contributing something to national prestige.

"Presenting the Red Arrows..."

At most air shows in Britain, the formal signal of the start of a Red Arrows display is the opening announcement, over the public address system, by the Team Manager/commentator:
"Good afternoon, ladies and gentlemen. May I present the Royal Air Force Aerobatic Team, the Red Arrows..."

And at that moment the nine Gnats sweep in from behind the crowd to go into their first manoeuvre, the arrival loop.

Although the team has introduced a number of new formations over the years, the basic framework for each season's display sequence is provided by formations which have established themselves as 'standards' in the Red Arrows repertoire. The pattern which provides the foundation for all the different formations is 'Diamond 9', from which the team flows into and out of the various formation changes. The Team Manager's deliberately low-key, undramatic commentary is intended chiefly to draw the spectators' attention to these formation changes before they actually take place.

Each year, therefore, the Red Arrows have mixed a fresh 'cocktail' for the air show public by combining standard formations and manoeuvres with new ones. What we have tried to do in the following pages is to construct photographically a representative 9-ship display sequence from our own 'cocktail' of formations and manoeuvres used by the Red Arrows in different seasons since 1965. Let's start, though, at a point before the team emerges into the view of the public...

About 15 minutes before take-off time, the Team Leader calls the pilots together for a final briefing on weather, wind strength and any important local data. They sign the necessary paperwork— even aerobatic teams aren't free from it!—then walk out to the waiting line of Gnats, where they are met by the groundcrew, who have already made their final inspection.

The nine pilots climb aboard, strap themselves in, and the canopies are closed. A quick last-minute check by every man—and the Red Arrows are ready for action...

With the aid of the team's two Palouste air starters, the Orpheus engines of the nine Gnats are started up in turn . . .

As the engines thunder into life, the groundcrews double round to the front of their respective aircraft to marshal them out . .

. . . and the Team Leader completes an R/T check of the whole team, then calls the control tower for clearance to taxi . . .

The Gnats taxi out in pairs at 50-yard intervals behind Red Leader, who calls up the tower for line-up to take off . . .

The leader calls: "Up to 90. Lights"—and, with 90 per cent power and landing lights on, the front five start to roll . . .

With the back four rolling off a couple of seconds after the front section, the Gnats gather speed and lift off the runway . . .

Airborne, the leader and front 'Vic' of five aircraft stay low, while the back four pull high to clear their slipstream...

As swiftly as possible after take-off, the back section closes on the front five to form 'Big 9' formation for the arrival loop . . .

Halfway up the loop, the team changes to 'Diamond 9', bends into a wing-over and comes back for the 'Diamond 9' barrel roll . . .

Another wing-over and, at its apex, the leader calls the change into 'Pyramid' for another formation loop...

Towards the top of the loop, the formation changes from 'Pyramid' back to 'Diamond 9' and the team begins a 360° turn ...

Halfway through the turn, at the farthest point from the crowd, Red Leader calls a formation change into 'Concorde' . . .

Pulling up into another loop, going away from the crowd, the formation changes yet again halfway up into 'Feathered Arrow'...

Out of the loop, into a wing-over, and then another change into 'Wineglass' for a formation roll along the line of the runway . . .

Into 'Arrow' for a loop, with the synchro pair splitting away, leaving seven Gnats (next page) to change to 'Vixen' for a bomb-burst...

An opposition loop by the synchro pair, Nos 6 and 7, is followed by a seven-ship roll in 'King's Cross' formation . . .

. . . then Nos 6 and 7 come in low, split and complete the 'Roulette' manoeuvre, passing each other at the datum point . . .

As the synchro pair disappears, the seven-Gnat section runs back down the runway in '7 Arrow' formation, and first Nos 2 and 3 . . .

. . . then Nos 4 and 5 simultaneously perform undercarriage rolls out of and back into their places in the formation . . .

As the main formation clears and changes formation, Nos 6 and 7 complete an opposition barrel roll, streaming white smoke...

Taking up echelon formation on the leader's port side, the seven Gnats of the main formation roll under to perform the 'Twizzle'...

Back come Nos 6 and 7 to cross in front of the crowd, half-roll off individual loops and cross each other again in the 'Boomerang' . . .

The seven-Gnat section returns for 'Leader's Benefit'.

Nos 6 and 7 sweep low across the airfield in their final synchro pair manoeuvre, the 'Undercarriage Roll'...

. . . for which the two aircraft stream different-coloured smoke, changing colours as they cross each other at datum . . .

Starting a loop in 'Leader's Benefit' then changing into 'Big 7', the main section plunges down in the 'Cascade' bomb-burst . . .

The nine Gnats sweep in from different directions, climbing to join up into a full 'Diamond 9' formation before the top of the loop . . .

A final 'Diamond 9' bend, then the final loop, with the formation breaking on the downswing into the 'Parasol' bomb-burst...

In the stream landing which closes the display—tail chutes being used when conditions dictate—last man to touch down is Red Leader.

In one word: teamwork...

Nobody could write about the Red Arrows and leave out the part played by the ground crews. Nine pilots do not make a team: it also needs some 60 NCOs and airmen whose work, though done mostly on the ground, is just as vital to success.

The demanding programme carried out by the Arrows over the last eight years or so would have been a total impossibility without superb standards of servicing and maintenance. For all that time, serviceability of the team's Gnats has been virtually 100 per cent. That is as much cause for pride as the actual flying, and it is a remarkable testimony to the skill, training and dedication of the ground staff.

Even if the aircraft were operating all year round from a permanent base, it would be a pretty impressive record. It is all the more impressive when one remembers that the Red Arrows are constantly on the move for the greater part of the display season, often operating from unfamiliar airfields and in foreign territory. In the space of months, the team can experience climatic conditions ranging from snow and frost to near-tropical heat—from English winters and the dubious delights of English springs to the sunny warmth of Malta or Cyprus, from Scottish mists to Mediterranean mistrals.

There can be very few European countries in which the team has not now displayed. Finland, Iceland and Austria have all been added in recent years, and in 1972 the Arrows crossed the Atlantic for the first time, giving displays in both Canada and the USA.

The Arrows evolved from the Yellowjacks who had ten Gnats with which to maintain a five-ship formation; today the team still has only ten Gnats but, since 1965, has consistently flown nine-ship formations. Only carefully planned and systematically executed servicing and maintenance could make that possible, however good the basic engineering qualities of the aircraft.

The Gnat is a first-class piece of engineering and the manufacturers, Hawker Siddeley, have given the Red Arrows maximum co-operation and assistance. But, in the final analysis, it is to the team's own engineering crews that the greatest credit belongs.

The major work of servicing and maintenance, plus whatever modifications the season may have called for, is done in the winter months between the stand-down of the team for annual leave in October and re-assembly for the new season in January. This is a particularly hardworking period for the Engineering Officer and his men but they have to be on their toes all through the season, too.

Experience has shown that, for every five days' flying, almost two days need to be allowed for work on the aircraft. On average, two of the ten Gnats are then likely to want the specialised attention and rectification which can be provided only at base at Kemble. As a result, the team normally stands down for two days on its return to base to allow rectification and scheduled servicing to be completed by the Engineering Wing personnel.

The Red Arrows' engineering team is split into two: a base ground crew and a travelling ground crew, both under the command of the Team Engineering Officer. The main responsibility for ensuring serviceability of the ten Gnats throughout the season rests with the base crew, which diagnoses and rectifies the larger faults, plans logistic requirements, and carries out the bulk of the engineering work.

The travelling crew, consisting of some 22 men under the Team Engineer Officer and a senior NCO, flies with the Arrows to every display away from base. In transit, the ten Gnats are flown by the nine display pilots and the Team Manager and each carries in its rear seat one of the ground crew. The remainder travel in a support aircraft—Argosy or Hercules—which also transports a basic range of spares and equipment sufficient to enable the team to operate away from base as a self-contained, self-sufficient unit.

There is a very close identification between individual ground crew members and individual aircraft. The name of the skilled tradesman assigned to each Gnat, in fact, is

The Red Arrows' most critical and appreciative spectators are their own ground crew, three members of which are seen assessing the station-keeping of the team in a 'Diamond 9' bend.

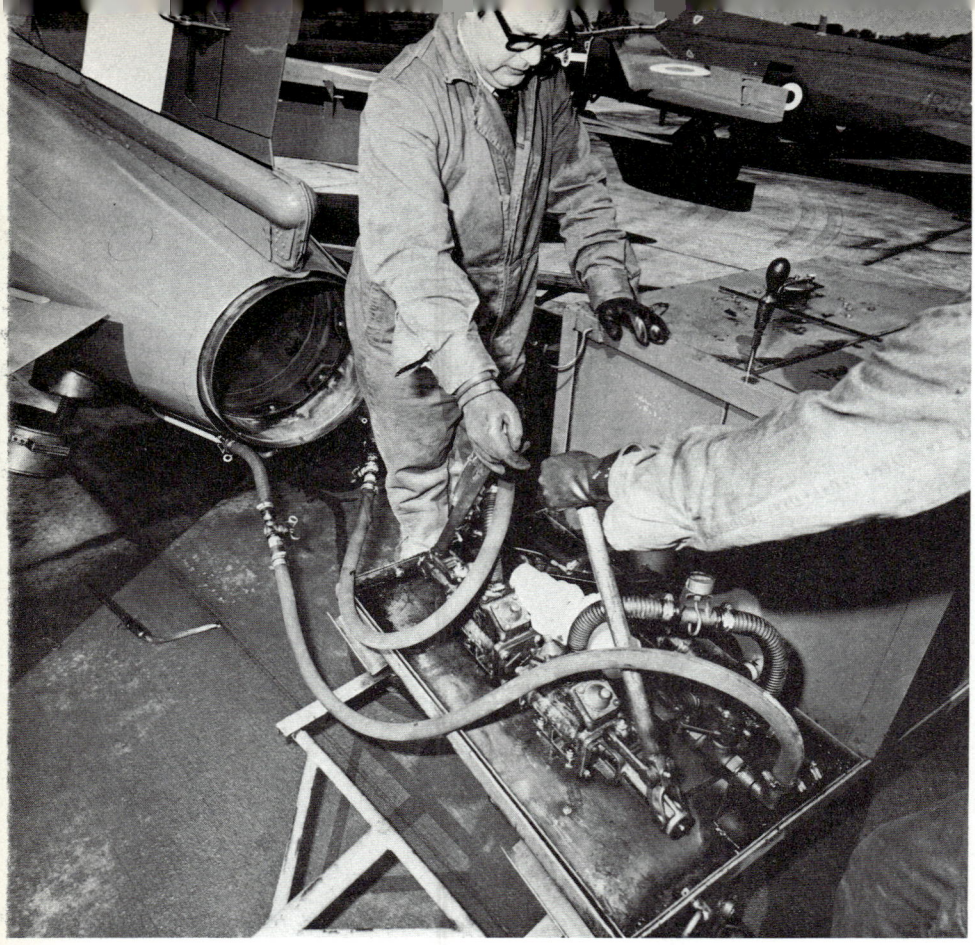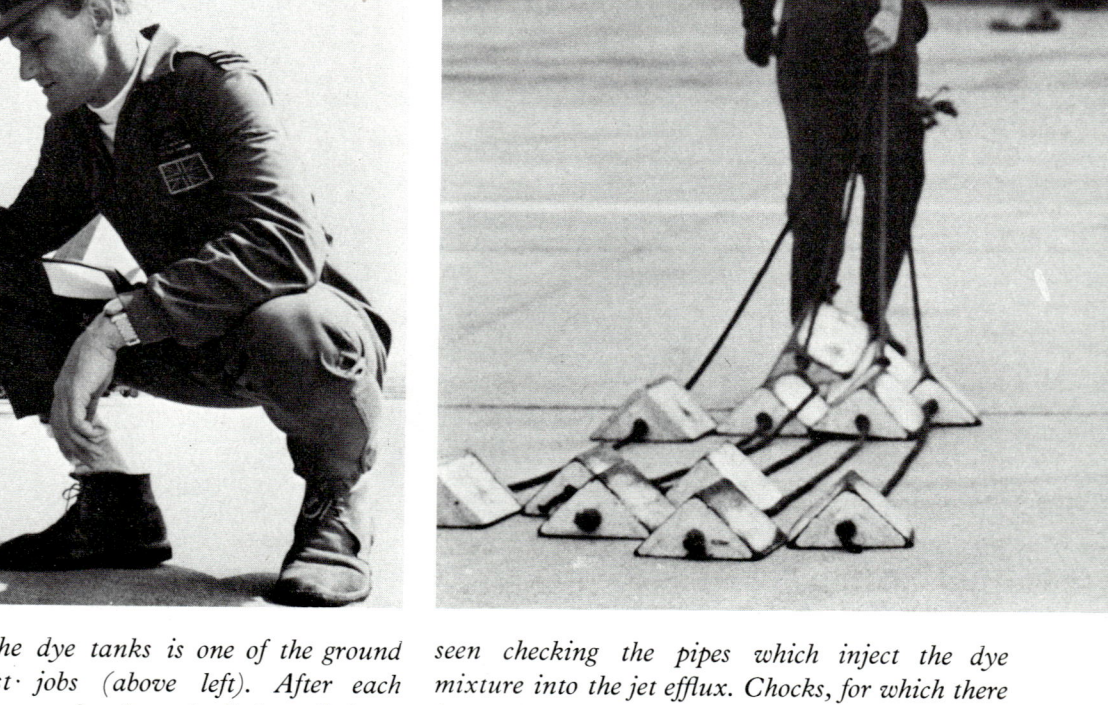

Replenishing the dye tanks is one of the ground crew's messiest jobs (above left). After each display, dye has to be cleaned off the tailplanes (above right). The team's Engineering Officer, Flight Lieutenant George White (below left), is seen checking the pipes which inject the dye mixture into the jet efflux. Chocks, for which there is no space in the Gnats on transit flights, are among the first items to be unloaded when the support aircraft arrives (below right).

Major servicing and maintenance tasks are carried out by the base ground crew at the Red Arrows' home base at Kemble, where a technician is seen working (above) on an Orpheus turbojet before re-installation in one of the Gnats.

lettered on the side of the fuselage below that of the pilot. Each technician feels a personal responsibility for his aircraft and regards it as being as much *his* Gnat as the pilot's. All of them guard jealously their right to fly with "their" Gnat and, to make way for the Engineer Officer, there is a strictly observed rota, by which each of the technicians stands down in turn.

The Engineer Officer therefore flies in each aircraft in turn. Journalists, photographers and other "guests" who occasionally fly with the team on transit are accommodated in the same way.

The fact that the Arrows operate away from base for so much of the time means that the ground crew of this "flying circus", as the other technicians call them, get considerably more flying than most RAF tradesmen, with the result that there is almost as much competition to join the team's ground staff as there is among pilots to become a member.

Whatever aspect of the Red Arrows you look at, you keep coming back to one word: teamwork. This is just as true of the ground operation as of the flying side. Every member of base and travelling crews is a highly trained and skilled tradesman, with clearly defined responsibilities—but everyone is also ready to lend a hand with any work outside his own area, whenever needed.

Team spirit shows itself in a number of ways, one of them being willingness to volunteer for the really dirty but necessary chores such as that of "dye merchant". Filling the dye tanks of the Gnat is a job which needs a good deal of care: there is nothing more irritating than to call for red smoke in a manoeuvre and find you have nothing but a messy smudge! It can also be an extremely messy job; once you get dye on your clothes or your skin, it isn't at all easy to remove.

But smoke makes all the difference to some manoeuvres, so somebody has to do the dirty work with the home-made "dye wagon"—and, typically, the lad who gets the job takes a fierce pride in it.

As a pilot with the Red Arrows, one very quickly develops a very high regard for the skill, ingenuity, capacity for hard work and

sheer enthusiasm of the ground crews, particularly when operating away from base on overseas visits.

Overseas displays became an important feature of the season almost from the very start of the Arrows. They help to make the year's programme an extremely complex organisation, involving an amount of planning and administrative work which few people outside the team could appreciate.

There is a steady stream of requests for the Arrows to take part in all kinds of displays at all kinds of venues, both at home and abroad. Some come direct to the team, some through the Ministry of Defence, some through HM Air Attachés overseas, some through other official channels. All the requests are reviewed at meetings of the Participation Committee at MoD, and eventually they are reduced to a manageable list which will allow as many shows as possible to be fitted into the season.

Detailed planning for the first display starts about six weeks before the actual event, when the display organiser is sent details of the team's logistic requirements, plus a supply of press and publicity material. Close contact is maintained with the organiser in following weeks by the Team Manager and Adjutant, who take care of the many minor problems which arise.

One week before the event, a military operation order is printed, setting out the final arrangements in detail—timings, transit arrangements and routes, personnel required, equipment needed, etc. The supporting Argosy or Hercules normally arrives at Kemble the day before the team departs to allow plenty of time to load spares, servicing equipment and personal kit.

Whenever possible, the team flies into the display airfield 24 hours before the actual show so that there is time for a practice on site. When the season is at its busiest, this is not always possible, however.

On arrival, the Team Leader, Team Manager and Engineer Officer meet the display organisers and airfield authorities to button up all final arrangements.

Top left, for transit flights the Gnats are fitted with slipper tanks which are not usually carried during display flying. Top right, one of the ground crew marshalling out one of the Gnats at Kemble. Below, ground crew of the 'travelling circus' supervise refuelling at an overseas airfield.

Even on transit flights, the Red Arrows know that they are very much in the public eye and never relax their standards of presentation. When possible and permissible, they give their arrivals a touch of showmanship with 'battle breaks' such as that over a French airfield in the top picture. At dispersal (below), the Gnats maintain a parade-ground perfection of line-up.

Over the season as a whole, the team is likely to fly four displays a week, most of them involving departure from Kemble on Thursday and return on Monday.

Fitting overseas displays into the season's framework naturally creates special problems. Not all the displays will actually be at airfields. Over the years, for instance, the Red Arrows have displayed in settings as various as the Nurburgring motor-racing circuit in Germany and the Brands Hatch circuit in Britain, over Valletta's Grand Harbour and the millionaires' yachts at Monte Carlo, and before crowds lining the seafronts of Brighton and Bari, Hastings and Nice, Jersey and Cannes, as well as at RAF stations and foreign air bases in many countries.

Quite often on the Continent, displays take place at well-used civil airports, and this demands tight timing by the team.

There was an occasion at Nice when our nine Gnats were about to do a "spaghetti break" into the circuit just as a Swissair pilot called the tower for clearance to land. The tower told him he was No 10 to land—which he naturally assumed to mean that there were nine procedure landings ahead of him. That would have meant about a 30-minute wait, and the Swissair man understandably started to protest forcibly to control about the lack of prior warning.

He had hardly opened his mouth when control came back and said: "It's OK—you're No 1 now."

In planning overseas visits, every attempt is made to group several displays together to form a logical week's itinerary. The transit arrangements are kept as flexible as possible because the Arrows' prime consideration is to make sure that the display goes on as planned. Weather which does not affect the Gnats can sometimes create problems for the support aircraft, which are not only a good deal slower but do not have the same ceiling.

Once agreement has been reached on the overseas displays to be included in the programme, and the airfields from which the team will operate are fixed, the first task is to decide on transit airfields for the Gnat and

Three of the many contrasting settings in which the Red Arrows display. Left: Biggin Hill typifies the 'showbiz' atmosphere of major public shows. Top: an advertising hoarding offers cryptic advice to Ernie Jones as he flies low over the Brands Hatch motor-race circuit! Lower picture: the team in 'Diamond 9' formation over the historic harbour walls of Malta's capital, Valletta, during a Mediterranean tour.

Top: most of the heavy load of administrative work involved in preparing for overseas visits falls to the Adjutant and Team Manager. Below: the team's support aircraft nowadays is usually a Hercules transport.

Even aerobatics display teams cannot escape official 'paperwork': lined up above waiting for the pilots' signatures are the aircraft acceptance documents known to generations of RAF personnel as '700s'.

the support aircraft. Agreement has to be reached with the appropriate authorities and organisations in the countries concerned, with the help of HM Air Attachés there, on the proposed operating plan.

A vast amount of detail has to be taken care of—show timings, transit timings and routes, diversion airfields, logistics, surface transport, accommodation and messing arrangements for pilots and ground crew, "official" social commitments and so on. It adds up to a lot of planning, paperwork and 'phone calls, most of it falling to the Team Manager and Adjutant.

The difference in performance between the Gnats and the support aircraft can make changes in the transit route a bit of a headache. It is then that the value of carrying technicians in the Gnat really becomes apparent. While waiting for the support aircraft to arrive, they can get on with jobs like removing the slipper tanks or clearing minor snags which might have shown up in transit. Time saved in this way can be invaluable with a tight programme.

There is no regular support aircraft assigned to the Red Arrows. An Argosy—disrespectfully christened the "Whistling Wheelbarrow" or "Argy-bomber" by the team's ground crews—or, more usually nowadays, a Hercules is allocated, as the need arises, from one of the RAF transport squadrons.

The Red Arrows' ground crews have brought the job of loading the transport aircraft to a fine art. To the casual onlooker, it may look like cheerful chaos but he will still be surprised at the speed with which the operation is completed. If he watched more closely, he would soon realise that everybody knows exactly what needs to be done, which bit of it he has to do, and precisely where everything needs to be stowed to make maximum use of the available hold space.

Sometimes it is possible to get the support aircraft away first from Kemble on a transit flight, so that their slower speed is less of a disadvantage. At most airfields, though, the Gnats need the Palouste air-starters to start their engines so that they have to leave first.

The Red Arrows usually transit in loose battle formation (upper picture) which contrasts strongly with the tightness of their display formations. Awaiting the arrival at Nice Airport of the slower support aircraft gives the pilots a rare opportunity to relax in the Riviera sunshine (lower picture).

This also means that the Gnats have to await the arrival of the transport aircraft at transit stops.

Normally, the Gnats themselves transit in two sections, with the aircraft flying in loose formation and No 6 leading the second section. When flying at high level, the aircraft are positioned so that the leader of each section can see all his aircraft at the same time and so that the Team Leader can also keep the whole of the second section in sight. At low level, No 6 drops further astern with his section, taking up a position so that his section is in deep echelon formation on the leader's section, with the individual aircraft also in deep echelon formation as a section. This makes sure that the leader has the freedom of manoeuvre necessary at lower altitudes, especially when approaching destination.

As a general rule, let-downs at the end of a transit stage are also made with the Gnats in close formation in two sections. If poor weather at destination means relying on runway approach aids, though, the team sometimes transits in sections of two or three aircraft with a 10-minute separation between sections.

Arrival may be the first sight that local people have of the team. Because the Arrows have always been firm believers in the value of making good first impressions, the team always aims at making a precise, polished job of landing, especially at overseas airfields where they know that critical eyes will be assessing their performance.

The normal technique is to land in stream at approximately 200-yard intervals, with alternate aircraft touching down left and right of the centre-line of the runway if the wind is straight on their noses. If there is a cross-wind, they land on the centre-line, with alternate aircraft moving left and right as they slow down so that the middle is kept clear for emergencies.

Top left: loading the supporting transport has been brought to a fine art by the team's ground crews. *Below left:* unloading in the hot sun of the French Riviera can be thirsty work.

Above: among the equipment which accompanies the team on overseas visits is the Land Rover seen above following the pilots' coach through the streets of Nice.

It is part of the "professionalism" of the Red Arrows that whenever they are flying as a team—even on transit flights—they are to all intents and purposes "on display". So, even on first arrival at a strange airfield, it has always been the practice to taxi back to dispersal in formation and shut down in unison. A minor detail, perhaps, but it is attention to minor details which gives the final polish to the team's performance.

Once at dispersal and out of the public eye, everybody relaxes. At transit stops, the pilots will sit on the grass and chat. The ground crew will check over the aircraft. If it is hot, they often strip down to a pair of swimming trunks—very practical wear although, when combined with flying boots, hardly the last word in sartorial elegance!

Really to appreciate the ground crew's gift for making the best of things, you need to fly with the 15 or so technicians who travel in the support aircraft. I cannot pretend that I have ever felt impelled to exchange my place in a Gnat for the delights of travelling in a heavily laden Argosy or Hercules but I have been told that the interior looks like a cross between a garage and a corner café!

Most of the hold is taken up with two vehicles —a short-wheelbase Land Rover and a Mini pick-up truck. The rest of the floor space is occupied by the dye wagon, the two Palouste engine starters, a back-end trolley for the Gnats, a very comprehensive home-built tool cabinet, and an inventory of spares which includes 17 mainwheels and four nose-wheels.

Every spare cubic inch of space is utilised for personal kit and baggage belonging to the pilots and ground staff. The vehicles are stuffed with bags and grips—only the favoured few are able to get a suit hung up inside the aircraft!

After the equipment is accommodated, what space is left is the ground crew's to enjoy. Paratroop seats are not exactly the last word in travel luxury but the NCOs and airmen have developed a remarkable ability to extract maximum comfort from these spartan assemblies of tubular framing and string netting. There are quieter places than the interiors of military transports, too, yet soon after take-off quite a few of the men occupying the seats against the fuselage walls on either side of the Land Rover are apt to be sound asleep!

From what I hear, it isn't long before somebody produces the inevitable, well-thumbed pack of cards and a school forms around the nose of the Land Rover. Hardened smokers say that the biggest drawback is that the presence in the hold of two vehicles, fuelled for the road, precludes "lighting up". In the Argosy, the nicotine addicts waited their turn to climb the ladder to the flight deck and stand, with their head and shoulders in the "office" upstairs, satisfying their craving for a cigarette.

Despite the informal, relaxed air that surrounds the ground crew, they form a highly disciplined unit. It is typical, for instance, that the NCOs always spend the early part of transit flights completing necessary paperwork—only afterwards will they relax with a book, snatch forty winks, or take a hand in the card game.

This kind of discipline comes from within the unit rather than being imposed from above. The fact is that the technicians are as proud as the pilots of being part of the RAF Aerobatic Team and know that their behaviour and performance contribute to the impression which outsiders form not only of the team but of the RAF as a whole—and even of Britain itself.

A tour of duty with the Arrows—invariably involving a number of trips overseas—is naturally a plum posting for a technician. On overseas trips, official invitations to receptions and the like are automatically regarded as including the ground staff. Because everybody is treated as part of the team, in fact, there are a spirit and loyalty which perhaps do more than anything else to ensure that— year in, year out—there is no falling off in the high serviceability which the Red Arrows' programme demands.

Squadron Leader Ray Hanna leading the Red Arrows over one of their best-known display venues—the SBAC Show at Farnborough.

The Arrows over home ground—the picturesque Cotswold town of Bourton-on-the-Water, close to the Central Flying School at Little Rissington.

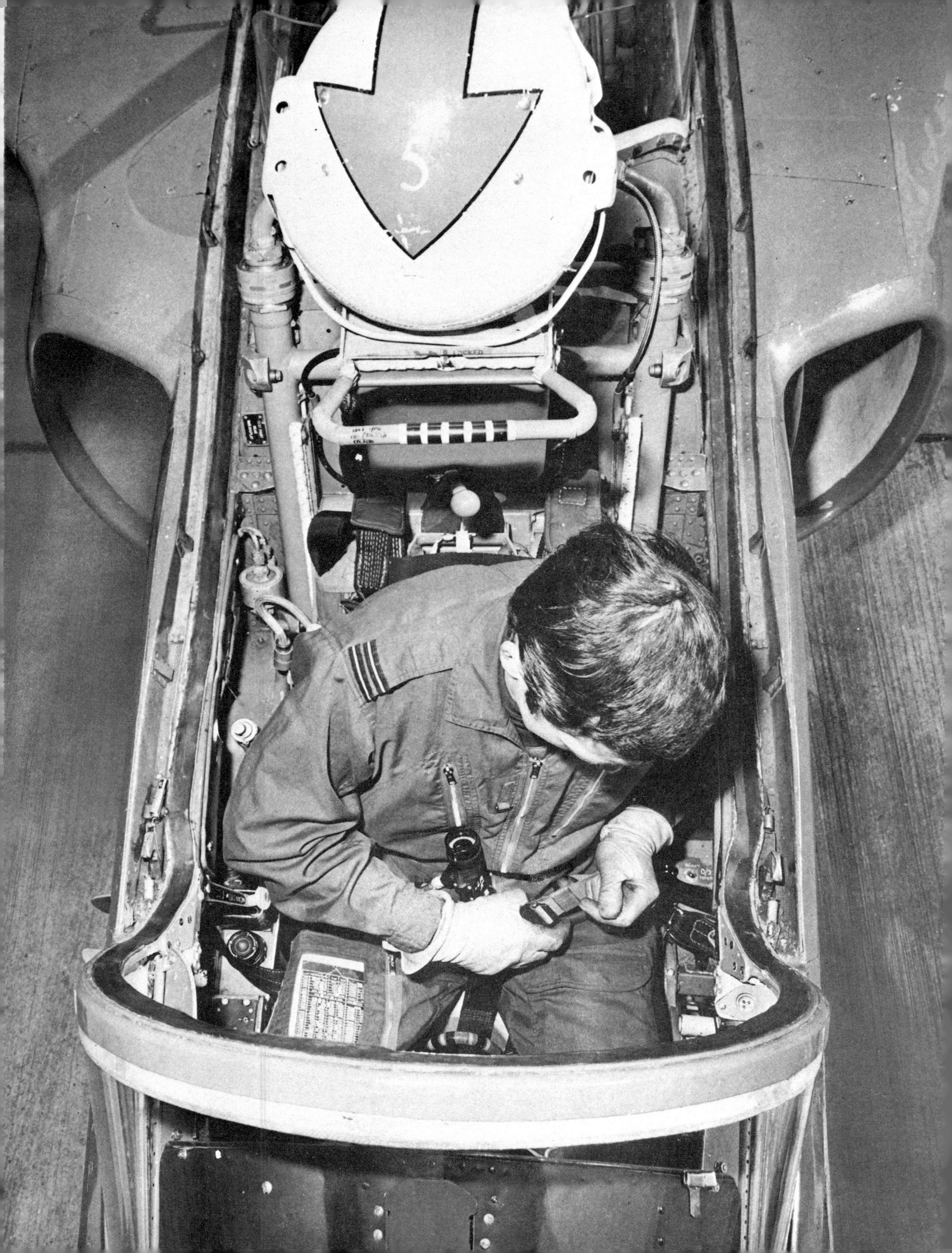

A classic aircraft

Every famous formation team has been closely identified with a particular type of aircraft, and there is no question that the RAF has been well served in having the Hawker Siddeley Gnat to equip its aerobatic team from 1965 onwards. In just about every respect—performance, manoeuvrability, controllability and sheer attractiveness of lines—this little trainer is virtually the ideal formation aerobatics aircraft. And you can add to those flying qualities, of course, the equally important quality of tremendous engineering reliability.

The Gnat T Mk 1 two-seat advanced trainer used by the Red Arrows was evolved from the earlier single-seat Gnat lightweight fighter designed by the Folland Aircraft team under the late W. E. W. Petter, which was first flown in 1955.

The original concept behind the design of the single-seat Gnat was to provide a small, economical fighter of good performance which could be built in quantity and put into the air in time of war in large numbers. Only two countries—Finland and India (where the aircraft was built under licence)—adopted the fighter version. In other countries, defence policy leaned towards larger, higher-powered, supersonic aircraft, preferring greater and more sophisticated all-round capability to availability in mass.

As a fighter, the Gnat was, in its day, a bold and original concept. It was approximately one-third of the weight and half the size of contemporary standard jet fighters and was designed to be manufactured without the aid of large and costly machine tools. Yet it had a high subsonic speed in level flight and transonic capability in a shallow dive with an exceptionally good rate of climb (essential in an aircraft intended primarily for interception) and a tight turning radius.

Although the RAF did not order the Gnat as a fighter, it did adopt the two-seat trainer version, first flown on August 31, 1959. A development order for 14 pre-production aircraft was placed in 1958, followed by contracts for a further 91 Gnats to replace the ageing Vampire T Mk 11 as the standard advanced trainer of the RAF Flying Training Schools.

Only two units were equipped with Gnats: the Central Flying School at Little Rissington (which received its first aircraft early in 1962) and No 4 Flying Training School at Valley (to which deliveries began in the autumn of 1962). The Gnats of the Central Flying School—both those allotted to its advanced jet training element and those assigned to the Red Arrows—operated on a detachment basis from RAF Fairford from 1965 to 1967 and then from RAF Kemble.

Compared with the single-seat version, the Gnat T Mk 1 has a lengthened fuselage to accommodate a second seat in tandem, and wings and tail unit of increased area. The trainer still handles like a fighter, however, and it can in fact be adapted to carry a variety of armament combinations.

The Gnat is very much a pilot's aircraft—highly manoeuvrable and a delight to handle, even in turbulent conditions close to the ground. Control is both crisp and super-sensitive, and on the particular variant used by the Red Arrows the rate of roll is especially good.

Tailplane and ailerons are power-operated, with an emergency facility for manual control. It is typical of the imaginative simplicity of the Gnat's design that there are no air brakes as such but partially extended undercarriage is used instead.

Although the basic structure of the aircraft is simple and easy to build, the standard of

The smallness of the Gnat's cockpit once prompted the remark: 'You don't so much get into a Gnat as pull it on'!

Left: general view of the tiny but efficient cockpit of the Gnat. Above: close-up views showing (top picture) the throttle quadrant and (lower picture) the VHF and UHF radio controls.

equipment is to a high level of sophistication and includes an integrated flight instrument system. Standby instruments are provided, the navigation display includes TACAN and ILS aids, and the aircraft has both VHF and UHF radio.

In the training role, the instructor has the rear seat, and both he and his pupil are accommodated in a pressurised cockpit with a one-piece jettisonable canopy. Both have Folland 4GT fully automatic lightweight ejector seats. Visibility from the cockpits is first-rate, and the aircraft can be flown by skilled, experienced instructors from the rear seat with a "passenger" in front. Many of Arthur Gibson's photographs in this book, in fact, were taken from the front seat of a Gnat and provide convincing evidence of the wide field of vision enjoyed by a pupil on this high-performance advanced trainer.

Power unit of the Gnat is the Rolls-Royce Orpheus turbojet, designed and built by what was originally the Bristol engine division and later Bristol-Siddeley, at Patchway just outside Bristol. The Orpheus is a straight-flow turbojet, with a seven-stage axial compressor driven by a single-stage turbine. It is as simple and robust in construction as the Gnat itself. Maximum rating of the engine is 4,520 lb static thrust at sea level.

There are three main differences between the standard RAF Gnats and those used by the Red Arrows.

The exceptional rate of roll which I mentioned earlier was made possible by the removal of the aileron stop. This allows double the normal aileron deflection for high-rate rolling. The aircraft is rolled only in the "clean" configuration (ie, with slipper tanks removed, gear raised, and flaps up) and, for stability reasons (roll/yaw couple), the aircraft is limited to one complete roll when full deflection is applied.

The removal of the slipper tanks is the second departure from the standard trainer configuration. The Gnat is flown "clean" in most displays, partly to allow the inclusion in the display sequence of maximum-rate rolls but also because the aircraft is more pleasant to fly in formation in this configuration.

These three far-from-drastic modifications apart, the Red Arrows' Gnats are essentially the same as the aircraft which, for ten years and more, have borne the brunt of the RAF's advanced jet pilot training programmes.

These high-rate rolls have always been a feature of the Arrows' display sequence, with manoeuvres like the "Twinkle Roll" when the aircraft roll simultaneously at a 400-degree/second rate of rotation.

The third difference between the team's Gnats and the standard trainers is the addition of a smoke-generation system. White smoke is made by injecting diesel oil by air pressure into the jet efflux immediately aft of the jet pipe, where the oil is vaporised. Approximately 30 gallons of diesel oil are carried in two tanks isolated for the purpose from the fuel system. However, a simple cock enables them to be converted back to fuel tanks when extra range is needed. It was this modification which made it possible for the team to cross the Atlantic and visit the USA and Canada in 1972.

With dye in the tanks and the slipper tanks removed for display purposes, of course, the range of the aircraft is limited.

There is a story among formation teams which may or may not be true but which has always struck a responsive chord with Red Arrow pilots. It refers to a bit of R/T "chat" which went: "Red 2 to Red Leader. I'm running short of fuel."

"Red Leader to Red 2. OK. Stick close to me—I've got plenty."

The dye mixture which provides the red and blue smoke is carried in two small additional "saddle" tanks, fitted aft, between the fuselage skin and the jet pipe.

The smoke systems are all electrically operated, the white by a switch on the throttle and the red and blue by two switches on the stick.

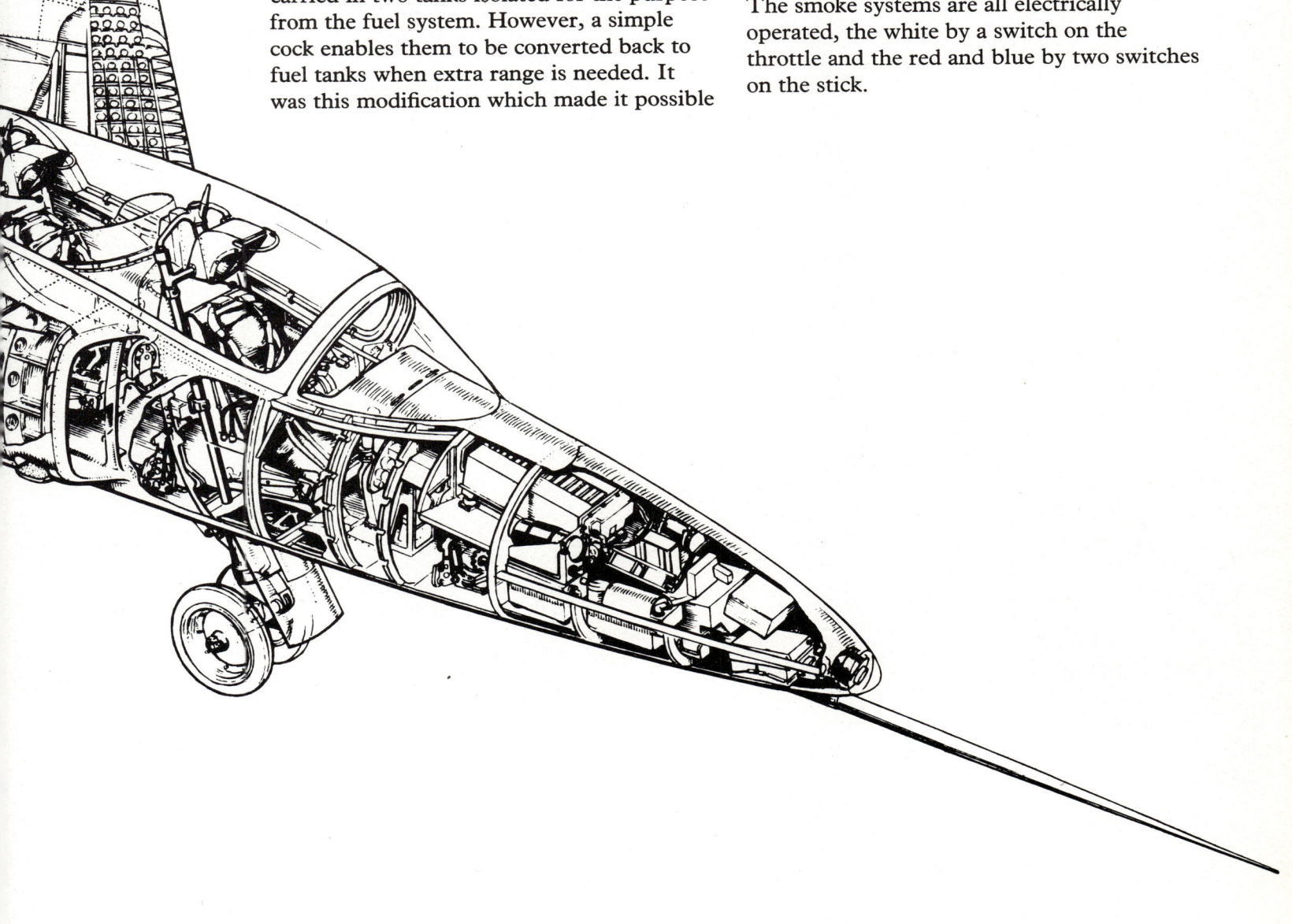

For those who like figures, it may be worth setting out the main technical data relating to the team's Gnats:

Maximum speed without slipper tanks:
sea level to 9,500 ft   Mach 0·92
above 9,500 ft   525 knots

Maximum speed with slipper tanks:
sea level to 11,000 ft   Mach 0·90
above 11,000 ft   500 knots

Maximum permissible
height   48,000 ft

Rate of climb, sea level to 40,000 ft:
without slipper tanks   7 mins
with slipper tanks   10 mins

Range (Red Arrows aircraft):
without slipper tanks   450 nautical miles
with slipper tanks   750 nautical miles

Maximum permissible g loadings:
positive   +7g
negative $-2\frac{1}{2}$g

Maximum weight for
take-off and all forms
of flying   9,350 lb

Maximum weight for
landing   7,850 lb

Principal dimensions:
overall length   37 ft 10 in
wing span   24 ft 0 in
height   10 ft 6 in
wheel track   5 ft 1 in

It is almost true, as somebody once said, that a pilot doesn't so much get into a Gnat as pull it on!

No recital of cold facts and figures, though, could do justice to an aircraft which has won the lasting affection and respect of so many pilots and which has inspired so many superb aerobatic display performances. For me, the Gnat is one of the classic aircraft designs of my flying era. It has been my good fortune to have been able to fly both the Gnat and that classic aircraft of an earlier generation, the Spitfire, in recent aerobatic displays, and I have often been asked to compare the two.

To a certain extent, comparisons must be unfair in view of the 30-year gap in their design technology. The Spitfire lacks the Gnat's control responsiveness and, of course, the sheer speed and smoothness of the jet. What it lacks in the technical and performance department, though, is more than made up for by its pure beauty of line— and certainly no one can even look at the Spitfire without being awed by the aura of history which will forever surround this fighter and its beautiful "crackling" Merlin engine. All aircraft, too, have their own distinctive smell—and none is quite as delicious as that of the Spitfire.

Faced with the choice of Gnat or Spitfire, I should unequivocally say: "Both, please!"

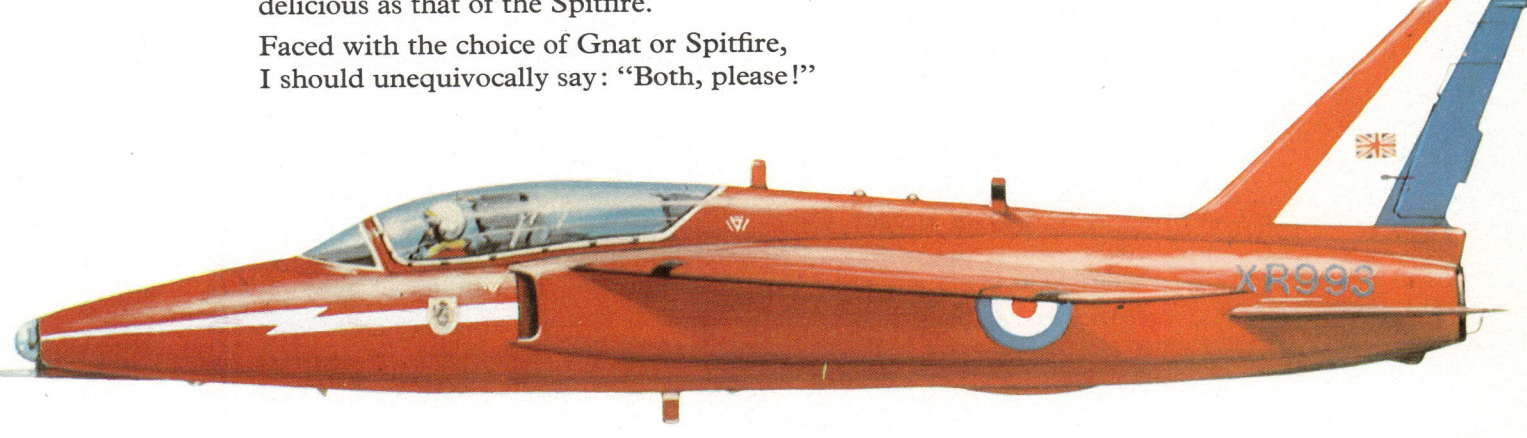

Individual individuals

The kind of piloting abilities demanded for membership of the Red Arrows inevitably means that most of the pilots have the same kind of Service background: fighter flying, with a fair amount of low-level experience, followed by a period as qualified flying instructors. Individually, however, they are as varied a bunch of men as you would be likely to find anywhere in the RAF. Most of them would stand out in any company, and, as I said in an earlier section of this book, they are all highly individual personalities.

The current leader, Ian Dick, for instance, captained the RAF ski team. Terry Kingsley and Peter Evans, two totally dissimilar personalities, formed an enterprising partnership outside the Arrows, competing in the London-Sydney and London-Mexico car marathons and in the London-Sydney and London-Victoria air races. In his unassuming way, in fact, Pete Evans is a man of quite remarkable individuality with what could be a unique record in having competed at top level as motor-cyclist, rally driver and air-race pilot!

People sometimes ask what happens to members of the Red Arrows after they complete their tours of duty with the team. The short answer is 'all kinds of things'. Nine years have passed since the team was established and, in the natural course of events, some of us have left the RAF. If there is one common motivation which we all share, it is, I suppose, the desire to go on flying, and those who have left the Service have begun new careers in commercial aviation.

Derek ('Dinger') Bell and Doug Smith, two of my former team-mates, have—like me—become airline pilots. Peter Evans is flying business aircraft with a Canadian operator.

The majority of Arrows pilots, though, have remained in the RAF and are scattered throughout the Service, some on ground postings, some on flying duties with operational squadrons. Tim Nelson, Terry Kingsley, Ernie Jones and Dicky Duckett are, at the time of writing, all with Lightning squadrons; Roy Booth with a Phantom squadron; Frank Hoare and Jack Rust with Harrier squadrons.

The enthusiasm for aerobatic flying will, without doubt, stay with all of us for as long as we live. I have been lucky enough to keep my hand in by flying one of the few surviving Spitfires in aerobatic displays. Henry Prince, one of the founder-members of the Arrows, found an outlet for his enthusiasm as Team Manager of RAF Leeming's two-ship aerobatic team, the Gemini. Roy Booth was flying again at Farnborough in 1970 as a member of a Phantom formation, and Jack Rust led the RAF Harrier team in the 1972 show.

The pages which follow are a kind of 'scrap-book' of nine years of the Red Arrows, a miscellany of photographs which includes group photographs of each year's teams. Interspersed with them are photographs of a few 'special events' and others which may help to make the point that Red Arrows teams, from 1965 onwards, have been a succession of very individual individuals!

Even on the ground, members of the Red Arrows show a flair for pastimes which call for precise handling at speed. Ian Dick (left) captained the RAF ski-ing team long before he became leader of the Arrows. Peter Evans (right) competed in the junior and senior Manx TT Races before joining the team in 1966.

1965

Team Leader	Flt. Lt. L Jones
No 2	Flt. Lt. B A Nice
No 3	Flt. Lt. R G Hanna
No 4	Flt. Lt. G L Ranscombe
No 5	Fg. Off. P G Hay
No 6	Flt. Lt. R E W Loverseed
No 7	Flt. Lt. H J D Prince
No 8	Flt. Lt. E C F Tilsley
Team Manager	Sqn. Ldr. R E Storer
Engineering Officers	Fg. Off. Harrow
	Fg. Off. Whitby

Ground Crew

FS. Hutson
Sgt. Scott
Sgt. Smallman
Cpl. Casey
Cpl. Chadburn
Cpl. Fernside
Cpl. Kellaher
Cpl. Mayes
Jnr. Tech. Austin
Jnr. Tech. Hardgreaves
Jnr. Tech. Howse
Jnr. Tech. Hurren
Jnr. Tech. Mearns
SAC. Arliss
SAC. Boucher
SAC. Dawson
SAC. Gannon
SAC. Green
SAC. Thomas

1966

Team Leader	Sqn. Ldr. R G Hanna
No 2	Flt. Lt. D A Bell
No 3	Flt. Lt. R W Langworthy
No 4	Flt. Lt. P R Evans
No 5	Flt. Lt. R Booth
No 6	Flt. Lt. H J D Prince
No 7	Flt. Lt. T J G Nelson
No 8	Flt. Lt. F J Hoare
No 9	Flt. Lt. D McGregor
Team Manager	Sqn. Ldr. R E Storer
Engineering Officers	Fg. Off. Harrow
	Fg. Off. Whitby

Ground Crew

FS. Hutson
Sgt. Thomas
Cpl. Chadburn
Cpl. Fernside
Cpl. Mayes
Cpl. Mearns
Cpl. Wood
Jnr. Tech. Austin
Jnr. Tech. Fennell
Jnr. Tech. Hardgreaves
Jnr. Tech. Howse
Jnr. Tech. Hurren
Jnr. Tech. Jones
Jnr. Tech. Scurr
Jnr. Tech. Steer
SAC. Boucher
SAC. Carroll
SAC. Dawson
SAC. Gannon
SAC. Green
SAC. Thomas

The Red Arrows, en route from the 1967 Paris show, pose for the camera with BAC One-Eleven destined for Aloha Airlines of Hawaii . . .

rthur Gibson's first photograph of the team, it illustrates the Arrows' readiness to aid the UK industry's export publicity efforts.

1967

Team Leader	Sqn. Ldr. R G Hanna
No 2	Flt. Lt. D A Bell
No 3	Flt. Lt. F J Hoare
No 4	Flt. Lt. P R Evans
No 5	Flt. Lt. R Booth
No 6	Flt. Lt. H J D Prince
No 7	Flt. Lt. E E Jones
Team Manager	Flt. Lt. L G Willcox
Adjutant	Flt. Lt. R Dench
Engineering Officer	Fg. Off. D Whitby

Ground Crew

FS. Hutson
Chf. Tech. Watson
Sgt. Thomas
Cpl. Bennett
Cpl. Chadburn
Cpl. Fletcher
Cpl. Nevard
Cpl. Smith
Cpl. Thomas
Cpl. Thurstans
Cpl. Turrell
Jnr. Tech. Austin
Jnr. Tech. Dalgleish
Jnr. Tech. Fennell
Jnr. Tech. Harris
Jnr. Tech. Howse
Jnr. Tech. McKnight
SAC. Carroll
SAC. Dunn
SAC. Gannon
SAC. Smith
SAC. Stidwill

Left: this shot of the Arrows over the 'white cliffs of Dover'—taken from a helicopter hovering about 300 ft above the sea—won the 'Financial Times' Export Award for Industrial Photography. The 'individualism' of the Arrows showed again when Terry Kingsley, Peter Evans and Derek Bell entered the London-Sydney Marathon in 1968 (top) and the first two later competed in the London-Mexico City Rally in 1970 (below).

1968

Team Leader	Sqn. Ldr. R G Hanna
No 2	Flt. Lt. D A Bell
No 3	Flt. Lt. D A Smith
No 4	Flt. Lt. P R Evans
No 5	Flt. Lt. F J Hoare
No 6	Flt. Lt. R Booth
No 7	Flt. Lt. J T Kingsley
No 8	Flt. Lt. I C H Dick
No 9	Flt. Lt. R B Duckett
Team Manager	Sqn. Ldr. L G Willcox
Adjutant	Flt. Lt. R Dench
Engineering Officer	Fg. Off. D Whitby

Ground Crew

Chf. Tech. Watson
Sgt. Souter
Sgt. Thomas
Cpl. Bennett
Cpl. Fletcher
Cpl. Nevard
Cpl. Smith
Cpl. Thomas
Cpl. Thurstans
Cpl. Turrell
Jnr. Tech. Austin
Jnr. Tech. Dalgleish
Jnr. Tech. Fennell
Jnr. Tech. Goodfellow
Jnr. Tech. Harding
Jnr. Tech. Harrington
Jnr. Tech. Harris
Jnr. Tech. Hudson
Jnr. Tech. Walters
SAC. Bell
SAC. Carroll
SAC. Jones
SAC. Pinkerton
SAC. Stidwill

The Red Arrows over Le Bourget Airport on the day in 1969 when the Paris air show drew its biggest-ever public attendance . . .

Below them, on the runway, is one of the main reasons for the record crowd—the Concorde prototype, making its public debut.

1969

Team Leader	Sqn. Ldr. R G Hanna
No 2	Flt. Lt. P R Evans
No 3	Flt. Lt. D A Smith
No 4	Flt. Lt. R B Duckett
No 5	Flt. Lt. E R Perreaux
No 6	Flt. Lt. J T Kingsley
No 7	Flt. Lt. I C H Dick
No 8	Flt. Lt. J D Rust
No 9	Sqn. Ldr. R P Dunn
Team Manager	Flt. Lt. P Mackintosh
Engineering Officer	Fg. Off. G E White
Adjutant	Flt. Lt. R Dench

Ground Crew

FS. Young
Chf. Tech. Loader
Chf. Tech. Souter
Sgt. Dicker
Sgt. Fowler
Sgt. Stuart
Cpl. Blight
Cpl. Harris
Cpl. Hudson
Cpl. Jones
Cpl. Perrett
Cpl. Sivell
Cpl. Thomas
Cpl. Turrell
Jnr. Tech. Fothergill
Jnr. Tech. Goodfellow
Jnr. Tech. Keyworth
Jnr. Tech. Scammell
SAC. Bell
SAC. Cresswell
SAC. Farra
SAC. Gannon
SAC. Hyland
SAC. Jones
SAC. Pinkerton
SAC. Williams

Above: the influence of the Red Arrows extends to other aerobatic teams. Founder-member Henry Prince was later Team Manager of the 'Gemini' team. Right: the Arrows displaying before HM the Queen and HRH Prince Charles at Little Rissington in 1969.

1970

Team Leader	Sqn. Ldr. D Hazell
No 2	Flt. Lt. E R Perreaux
No 3	Flt. Lt. D A Smith
No 4	Flt. Lt. J D Rust
No 5	Flt. Lt. J Haddock
No 6	Flt. Lt. I C H Dick
No 7	Flt. Lt. R B Duckett
No 8	Flt. Lt. D S B Marr
No 9	Flt. Lt. R E W Loverseed
Team Manager	Flt. Lt. P Mackintosh
Engineering Officer	Flt. Lt. G E White
Adjutant	WO. L Ludlow

Ground Crew

FS. Arthur
Chf. Tech. Dicker
Chf. Tech. Fowler
Chf. Tech. Francis
Chf. Tech. Souter
Chf. Tech. Thomas
Sgt. Blight
Sgt. Turrell
Cpl. Goodfellow
Cpl. Jones
Cpl. Scammell
Cpl. Sivell
Jnr. Tech. Heeley
Jnr. Tech. Lagor
SAC. Bell
SAC. Cresswell
SAC. Crewe
SAC. Farra
SAC. Frampton
SAC. Gannon
SAC. O'Brian

In the England-Australia air race at the end of 1969, Terry Kingsley, Peter Evans and Arthur Gibson had the unwelcome distinction of providing the biggest news story when their SIAI Marchetti SF260 was forced down on a remote Indonesian island beach by violent storms. With the aid of islanders, a palm-leaf runway was improvised on the soft sand to enable Kingsley to take off and fly to an airfield, where his companions rejoined him to complete the race.

In the London-Victoria (BC) air race in 1971, Peter Evans, Terry Kingsley and Arthur Gibson formed the crew of a Britten-Norman Islander, on delivery to a Canadian distributor, and finished 13th of 57 starters. Over Victoria, Gibson took this air-to-air shot of the four Britten-Norman aircraft which competed—three Islanders (with No 54, their own aircraft, nearest camera) and the Trislander, which made its first-ever Transatlantic crossing in the course of the race.

1971

Team Leader	Sqn. Ldr. R E W Loverseed
No 2	Sqn. Ldr. D S B Marr
No 3	Flt. Lt. A C East
No 4	Flt. Lt. W B Aspinall
No 5	Flt. Lt. P J J Day
No 6	Flt. Lt. C F Roberts
No 7	Flt. Lt. R E Somerville
Team Manager	Flt. Lt. K J Tait
Engineering Officer	Flt. Lt. G E White
Adjutant	WO. L Ludlow

Ground Crew

FS. Fisk
Chf. Tech. Dicker
Chf. Tech. Fowler
Chf. Tech. Souter
Chf. Tech. Thomas
Sgt. Baker
Sgt. Stuart
Cpl. Armstrong
Cpl. Audley
Cpl. Hudson
Cpl. Jones
Cpl. Lawrence
Cpl. Perrett
Cpl. Scammell
Cpl. Webb
Jnr. Tech. Heeley
Jnr. Tech. Lagor
Jnr. Tech. Ruffle
SAC. Bell
SAC. Cresswell
SAC. Frampton
SAC. Gannon
SAC. Goddard
SAC. Howard
SAC. Marsh
SAC. Shorter
SAC. Thompson

The Harrier formation which displayed at Farnborough in 1972, under the leadership of ex-Arrow pilot Jack Rust, above the Gnat of the 1972 team leader, Squadron Leader Ian Dick, awaiting clearance for take-off.

Not leaping dolphins but a formation of Phantoms rehearsing for their contribution to the 1970 SBAC show at Farnborough. Pilot of Arthur Gibson's photographic aircraft on this occasion and a member of the Farnborough formation was ex-Arrow pilot Roy Booth.

1972

Team Leader	Sqn. Ldr. I C H Dick
No 2	Flt. Lt. W B Aspinall
No 3	Flt. Lt. A C East
No 4	Flt. Lt. R E Somerville
No 5	Flt. Lt. K J Tait
No 6	Flt. Lt. P J J Day
No 7	Flt. Lt. D Binnie
No 8	Flt. Lt. E E G Girdler
No 9	Flt. Lt. C F Roberts
Team Manager	Flt. Lt. B Donnelly
Engineering Officer	Flt. Lt. I Brackenbury
Adjutant	WO. S Wild

Ground Crew

FS. Fisk
Chf. Tech. Dicker
Chf. Tech. Fowler
Chf. Tech. Martin
Chf. Tech. Shea
Sgt. Ransom
Sgt. Sampson
Cpl. Armstrong
Cpl. Hudson
Cpl. Lawrence
Cpl. Perkin-Ball
Cpl. Potter
Cpl. Scammell
Cpl. Walton
Cpl. Webb
Jnr. Tech. Blandford
Jnr. Tech. Ruffle
SAC. Bell
SAC. Cresswell
SAC. Goddard
SAC. Marsh
SAC. Radge
SAC. Shorter
SAC. Tarte
SAC. Worthington

In 1972, the Red Arrows realised an ambition almost as old as the team itself: a visit by the full team to the USA and Canada.

For 'Operation Longbow', as the project was named, the rear middle tanks of the Gnats were modified to take either aviation fuel or diesel oil for smoke generation. Two Hercules transports were allocated to carry groundcrew and spares for the 5-weeks tour—the longest period the team had ever been away from its home-base servicing facilities. Detachment Commander was the Commandant of CFS, Air Commodore Roy Crompton.

Led by Squadron Leader Ian Dick, the ten Gnats left Kemble on May 15th and—flying via Lossiemouth, Stornoway, Keflavik, Sondrestrom, Frobisher and Goose Bay—were shepherded across the North Atlantic by two Vulcans of Strike Command. Most of the flight was made at Mach 0·81 at 40,000 ft. When asked later how they had flown the Gnats to Canada, one of the pilots replied, with the laconic humour typical of the Arrows: "Very carefully!"

Practice sorties at Trenton, HQ of Canada's Air Transport Command, brought the team to concert pitch for its visit to the huge 'Transpo '72' exhibition at Dulles Airport, Washington. Between May 26th and June 2nd, before crowds estimated to total 1·5 million, the Arrows gave a series of performances which a senior British officer later said had 'done much to restore British aviation prestige in North America'.

Further displays were given at Reading, Pennsylvania, before the team flew back to Canada for shows at Bagotville fighter base, at Trenton, and at the Niagara District Airport at St Catherines, from which the Arrows had earlier overflown the famous Falls for the benefit of photographers.

'Operation Longbow' ended with the return crossing of the Atlantic, this time overflying Stornoway and bringing the Red Arrows triumphantly back to their home base at Kemble on June 16th.

1973

Team Leader	Sqn. Ldr. I C H Dick
No 2	Sqn. Ldr. W B Aspinall
No 3	Flt. Lt. B Donnelly
No 4	Flt. Lt. E E G Girdler
No 5	Flt. Lt. K J Tait
No 6	Flt. Lt. D Binnie
No 7	Flt. Lt. R E Somerville
No 8	Flt. Lt. D J Sheen
No 9	Flt. Lt. P J J Day
Team Manager	Flt. Lt. R M Joy
Engineering Officer	Flt. Lt. I Brackenbury
Adjutant	WO. H E D Rundstrom

Ground Crew

FS. Fisk
Chf. Tech. Hosking
Chf. Tech. Martin
Chf. Tech. Shea
Sgt. Dalgleish
Sgt. Ransom
Sgt. Sampson
Cpl. Armstrong
Cpl. Hudson
Cpl. Marson
Cpl. Perkin-Ball
Cpl. Potter
Cpl. Scammell
Cpl. Walton
Cpl. Webb
Jnr. Tech. Blandford
Jnr. Tech. Lee
Jnr. Tech. Ruffle
SAC. Bell
SAC. Chandler
SAC. Clay
SAC. Cresswell
SAC. Dallison
SAC. Radge
SAC. Shorter
SAC. Vale
SAC. Worthington

The Red Arrows' influence once again: this shot of two Lightnings of No 92 Squadron making a reheat break was photographed by Arthur Gibson from a third Lightning flown by former team-member Terry Kingsley.

Ray Hanna flying a Spitfire—like the Gnat, a classic aircraft in its own generation—over the team which he led for so long at the Biggin Hill Air Fair.

Postscript

In his foreword, Air Vice-Marshal Ivor Broom has been embarrassingly complimentary about me. The real credit for what the Red Arrows have achieved, however, does not belong to any one individual but to the Service as a whole.

It was the decision of the Royal Air Force to set up and maintain a full-time aerobatic team which made it all possible. It is the RAF's standards of training and discipline which have produced the pilots and groundcrews who have taken the team from success to success. These are the people who really made this book, and Arthur Gibson and I count ourselves fortunate to have been able to work with them.

If I were to attempt to express my personal thanks to all those to whom I feel a debt of gratitude, the list would be almost endless. There are a few names, however, which I would like to single out for individual mention because of all they did, in my time with the Arrows, to help the team to get established and whose backing meant so much to me.

All through the Red Arrows' history, one of the most important factors in the team's success has been the constancy of support we have received from the staff of the Central Flying School, from the AOC and Commandant downwards. All the people who served with me in the team have good cause to remember the successive Commandants under whom we served, all Air Commodores then but now all deservedly elevated to the rank of Air Vice-Marshal: Air Vice-Marshal H. A. C. Bird-Wilson, Air Vice-Marshal F. L. Dodd and, of course, Air Vice-Marshal Broom.

Among others who gave us a lot of support in the early days were the Station Commander at Little Rissington, Group Captain J. F. J. Dewhurst, who later retired with the rank of Air Commodore, and the 'Wingco Engineering', now Air Commodore G. E. Thirlwall.

There are three people outside the RAF, too, whom I have good reason to remember with gratitude: Gordon Hodgson, of Hawker Siddeley's design staff; Jack Buchanan, Hawker Siddeley's Gnat field representative; and Arthur Goody, his opposite number on the Orpheus with Bristol Siddeley/Rolls Royce.

Perhaps most of all, though, I owe my thanks to the man who started it all: Lee Jones.

To all those others I have not named, though, I should like to say that this book is in part my tribute to all you did to make the Red Arrows a success. For all of us, the greatest source of satisfaction, I am sure, is that the Red Arrows continue to go from strength to strength. I hope they will do so for many years to come.

Ray Hanna

As an outsider who had the good fortune to be welcomed into the Red Arrows, I am perhaps even more acutely conscious than Ray Hanna of the debt of gratitude I owe to a whole host of people, both inside and outside the Royal Air Force. Ray has named some of them but there are others I would like to add.

They start, of course, with Ray Hanna himself—and Tim Nelson who first introduced me to him at the 1967 Paris air show. The list could run through all the leaders and members of the team from then down to Ian Dick and the present-day team. If I single out Peter Evans and Terry Kingsley from among all the pilots for special mention, it is simply because competing in two international air races brought us particularly close together.

I have every reason to second what Ray has said about the Commandants and staff of the Central Flying School. The kindness which was shown to me by those whom Ray has named has been continued by two later Commandants, Air Commodore F. S. Hazlewood (now Air Vice-Marshal) and the present holder of the post, Air Commodore Roy Crompton, and his Station Commander, Group Captain Bob Barndon.

This is an opportunity, too, for me to place on record my appreciation of all the co-operation I have enjoyed from the RAF public relations staff at the Ministry of Defence under Air Commodore Peter Brothers and his successor as DPR (RAF), Air Commodore Paddy Forsyth. Like most public relations departments, 'MoD PR' probably collects more brickbats than bouquets, so I am glad to be able to redress the balance a little. And, for the same reason, I would like to add my thanks to David Bainbridge of Hawker Siddeley's PR staff.

Finally, there are two of my own colleagues without whom production of this book would have been impossible: Stan Edwards and Wally Pyemont. Like Ray, I should like to say to them and to all the others I have left unnamed:

'This book is as much yours as ours'.

Arthur Gibson

Acknowledgements

Lesley Craig	Typography & Layout
Flight International	Cutaway drawing on pages 134/5
Derek Bunce	3-view drawings on pages 136/7

We gratefully acknowledge photographs from the following sources:

Pages:—

Flight International	8, 10, 12, 14, 18 (top)
British Aircraft Corporation	18 (bottom)
Unknown photographers	20, 26 (top left), 139, 149
Rolls-Royce (Bristol Siddeley)	23
United States Air Force	27 (bottom)
Ministry of Defence	28 (bottom), 29 (bottom), 41 (top right), 140/1, 142/3, 154/5, 158/9, 170/1
John Rigby	33, 162/3, 166/7
Wally Pyemont	64
Red Arrows team photographers	68 (bottom left), 121 (top right)
RAF Luqa, Malta	95, 99
Richard Wilson	113
J. G. Frendo, Malta	121
Peter Stevenson, MoD (RAF)	168/9